JESUS SAID

Compiled by
Ronald Philipchalk
and
Phillip H. Wiebe

THOMAS NELSON PUBLISHERS

Nashville

Published in Nashville, Tennessee, by Thomas Nelson, Inc., and distributed in Canada by Lawson Falle, Ltd., Cambridge, Ontario.

Scripture quotations are from the NEW KING JAMES VERSION of the Bible. Copyright © 1979, 1980, 1982, Thomas Nelson, Inc., Publishers.

**Library of Congress
Cataloging-in-Publication Data**

Bible. N.T. Gospels. English. New King James. Selections. 1990.
    Jesus said / [compiled by] Ronald Philipchalk and Philip H. Wiebe.
        p. cm.
    A compilation of Jesus' words from the four Gospels and the book of Acts.
    ISBN 0-8407-7451-6
    1. Jesus Christ—Words. I. Philipchalk, Ronald P., 1945–
II. Wiebe, Phillip H., 1945– . III. Bible. N.T. Acts. English. New King James. Selections. 1990. IV. Title.
BS2553.P45 1990
226′.052036—dc20   90-33011
                                                          CIP

Printed in the United States of America
1 2 3 4 5 6 7 — 95 94 93 92 91 90

CONTENTS

On Himself

His Identity	13
Spiritual Food and Drink	14
The Good Shepherd	17
The Light of the World	18
The Life	19
His Authority	20
His Relationship to the Father	25
His Mission	28
The Fulfillment of Prophecy	33

Teachings

The Beatitudes	37
Warnings	38
The New Birth	39
Eternal Life	40
The Pre-eminence of God	43
Deeds Rewarded	44
The Importance of Guarding One's Speech	47
Children	48
Marriage and Divorce	50
Riches	52
Bearing Fruit	54
Taxes and Tribute	56
Hell	57

Thoughts and Behavior   58

Commitment   60

Submission   62

Trust   65

Worship   67

Religious Practices   68

Faith   70

Love and Obedience   74

Reproof and Forgiveness   77

Giving   79

The Proper Role of the Law   80

The Holy Spirit   82

Evil Spirits   83

Warning Against Signs   84

The Kingdom of God   86

   Entering the Kingdom   86

   Position in the Kingdom   88

   Perceiving the Kingdom   91

Promises to His Followers

Authority   95

The Holy Spirit   97

Peace and Rest   100

A Place in Heaven   101

Rewards   102

Inheritance   103

Prayer

Teaching on Prayer   107

His Own Prayers   109

Admonitions and Exhortations

Calling His Disciples   115

Charge to His Disciples   116

Harsh Words for the Religious System   119

Laments for the Cities of Israel   129

Judgment   131

Words on the Cross   132

Predictions

His Rejection and Death   137

His Resurrection   142

His Ascension and Glorification   143

Persecution of His Followers   146

The Resurrection of the Saints   149

His Coming in Glory   151

The End of the Age   153

Various Other Predictions   159

Parables

The Radical Nature of His Message   163

    The New and the Old Wineskins   163

The Response to His Message   164

    The Sower   164

His Rejection 166
   The Wicked Tenants 166
Being Prepared for the End 167
   Wise and Foolish Builders 167
   Marriage Guest Ejected 167
   The Ten Virgins 168
   The Foolish Rich Man 169
Stewardship and Bearing Fruit 171
   Good and Bad Stewards 171
   The Fig Tree 172
   The Clever but Evil Steward 173
Obedience 175
   The Two Sons 175
True Religion 176
   The Good Samaritan 176
   The Pharisee and the Tax-Collector 177
Value of Membership in the Kingdom 178
   Treasure in a Field 178
   The Pearl of Great Price 178
   Treasures Old and New 178
Growth of the Kingdom 179
   The Mustard Seed 179
   Leaven 179
   Natural Growth 179
Forgiveness 181
   The Unjust Servant 181

Forgiven Much, Forgiven Little — 182

The Prodigal Son — 183

The Last Shall Be First — 185

The Laborer's Wages — 185

The Guests' Excuses — 186

The Rich Man and Lazarus — 187

The End of the Age — 189

The Wheat and the Tares — 189

Good and Bad Fish — 190

The Unrighteous Judge — 190

PREFACE

"The greatest teacher who ever lived," "charlatan," "religious fanatic," "the Son of God"; these are a few of the epithets which have been applied to Jesus of Nazareth. No other individual has so affected the course of history. Yet He wrote no books, cut no records, produced no films or videos. The closest tangible link we have with Him is a few hundred words recounted by three of His close companions (Matthew, John, and Peter through Mark) and Luke, who was the companion of Paul—one of Jesus' greatest missionaries.

It was our belief that these words possess continued potency that prompted us to collect them in their present format—a compilation and arrangement into categories of virtually all the words of Jesus recorded in the four Gospels and the book of Acts. Overlap among the various accounts has been eliminated, with the most complete statement being presented where more than one is available. The only omissions are short phrases or statements which were parts of conversations and would not meaningfully stand alone. We have chosen the New King James Version because of its accuracy, readability, and beauty.

It is our hope that in reflecting on these words of Jesus as they are presented here, you will be struck anew, as we were, by their freshness and poignancy.

June 1990   Ronald Philipchalk
                                             Phillip H. Wiebe

ON HIMSELF

His Identity

ॐ

[*To Peter, who has called Him the Christ, the Son of the living God*]

Blessed are you, Simon Bar-Jonah, for flesh and blood has not revealed this to you, but My Father who is in heaven.

(Matthew 16:15–17; cf. Matthew 11:4–6, Luke 7:22–23, 24:26)

[*To the High Priest who asked if He was the Christ, the Son of God*]

It is as you said. Nevertheless, I say to you, hereafter you will see the Son of Man sitting at the right hand of the Power, and coming on the clouds of heaven.

(Matthew 26:64; cf. Mark 14:62, Luke 22:67–70)

How can they say that the Christ is the Son of David? Now David himself said in the Book of Psalms: "The Lord said to my Lord, 'Sit at My right hand, till I make Your enemies Your footstool.'" Therefore David calls Him "Lord"; how is He then his Son?

(Luke 20:41–44; cf. Matthew 22:41–45, Mark 12:35–37)

Your father Abraham rejoiced to see My day, and he saw it and was glad. Most assuredly, I say to you, before Abraham was, I AM.

(John 8:56, 58)

Do you believe in the Son of God? You have both seen Him and it is He who is talking with you.

(John 9:35, 37)

My kingdom is not of this world. If My kingdom were of this world, My servants would fight, so that I should not be delivered to the Jews; but now My kingdom is not from here.

(John 18:36–37)

Spiritual Food and Drink

[*At the Last Supper*]

[*Concerning the bread*] Take, eat; this is My body. [*Concerning the cup*] Drink from it, all of you. For this is My blood of the new covenant, which is shed for many for the remission of sins.

(Matthew 26:26–28; cf. Mark 14:22–24, Luke 22:19–20)

If you knew the gift of God, and who it is who says to you, "Give Me a drink," you would have asked Him, and He would have given you living water. Whoever drinks of this water will thirst again, but whoever drinks of the water that I shall give him will never thirst. But the water that I shall give him will become in him a fountain of water springing up into everlasting life.

(John 4:10, 13, 14)

Most assuredly, I say to you, Moses did not give you the bread from heaven, but My Father gives you the true bread from heaven. For the bread of God is He who comes down from heaven and gives life to the world.

(John 6:32–33)

I am the bread of life. He who comes to Me shall never hunger, and he who believes in Me shall never thirst. But I said to you that you have seen Me and yet do not believe. All that the Father gives Me will come to Me, and the one who comes to Me I will by no means cast out. For I have come down from heaven, not to do My own will, but the will of Him who sent Me. This is the will of the Father who sent Me, that of all He has given Me I should lose nothing, but should raise it up at the last day. And this is the will of Him who sent Me, that everyone who sees the Son and believes in Him may have everlasting life; and I will raise him up at the last day. No one can come to Me unless the Father who sent Me draws him; and I will raise him up at the last day. It is written in the prophets, "And they shall all be taught by God." Therefore everyone who has heard and learned from the Father comes to Me. Not that

anyone has seen the Father, except He who is from God; He has seen the Father. Most assuredly, I say to you, he who believes in Me has everlasting life. I am the bread of life. Your fathers ate the manna in the wilderness, and are dead. This is the bread which comes down from heaven, that one may eat of it and not die. I am the living bread which came down from heaven. If anyone eats of this bread, he will live forever; and the bread that I shall give is My flesh, which I shall give for the life of the world.
(John 6:35–40, 44–51)

Most assuredly, I say to you, unless you eat the flesh of the Son of Man and drink His blood, you have no life in you. Whoever eats My flesh and drinks My blood has eternal life, and I will raise him up at the last day. For My flesh is food indeed, and My blood is drink indeed. He who eats My flesh and drinks My blood abides in Me, and I in him. As the living Father sent Me, and I live because of the Father, so he who feeds on Me will live because of Me. This is the bread which came down from heaven—not as your fathers ate the manna, and are dead. He who eats this bread will live forever.
(John 6:53–58)

If anyone thirsts, let him come to Me and drink. He who believes in Me, as the Scripture has said, out of his heart will flow rivers of living water.
(John 7:37–38)

The Good Shepherd

Most assuredly, I say to you, he who does not enter the sheepfold by the door, but climbs up some other way, the same is a thief and a robber. But he who enters by the door is the shepherd of the sheep. To him the doorkeeper opens, and the sheep hear his voice; and he calls his own sheep by name and leads them out. And when he brings out his own sheep, he goes before them; and the sheep follow him, for they know his voice. Yet they will by no means follow a stranger, but will flee from him, for they do not know the voice of strangers. Most assuredly, I say to you, I am the door of the sheep. All who ever came before Me are thieves and robbers, but the sheep did not hear them. I am the door. If anyone enters by Me, he will be saved, and will go in and out and find pasture. The thief does not come except to steal, and to kill, and to destroy. I have come that they may have life, and that they may have it more abundantly. I am the good shepherd. The good shepherd gives His life for the sheep. But a hireling, he who is not the shepherd, one who does not own the sheep, sees the wolf coming and leaves the sheep and flees; and the wolf catches the sheep and scatters them. The hireling flees because he is a hireling and does not care about the sheep. I am the good shepherd; and I know My sheep, and am known by My own. As the Father knows Me, even so I know the Father; and I lay down my life for the sheep. And other sheep I have which are not of this fold; them also I must bring, and they will hear My voice; and there will be one flock and one shepherd. Therefore My Father loves Me, because I lay down My life that I may take it again. No one takes it from Me, but I lay it down of Myself. I have power to lay it down, and I have power to take it again. This command I have received from My Father.

(John 10:1–18)

But you do not believe, because you are not of My sheep, as I said to you. My sheep hear My voice, and I know them, and they follow Me. And I give them eternal life, and they shall never perish; neither shall anyone snatch them out of My hand. My Father, who has given them to Me, is greater than all; and no one is able to snatch them out of My Father's hand.

(John 10:26–29)

The Light of the World

I am the light of the world. He who follows Me shall not walk in darkness, but have the light of life.

(John 8:12)

I must work the works of Him who sent Me while it is day; the night is coming when no one can work. As long as I am in the world, I am the light of the world.

(John 9:4–5)

Are there not twelve hours in the day? If anyone walks in the day, he does not stumble, because he sees the light of this world. But if one walks in the night, he stumbles, because the light is not in him.
(John 11:9–10)

A little while longer the light is with you. Walk while you have the light, lest darkness overtake you; he who walks in darkness does not know where he is going. While you have the light, believe in the light, that you may become sons of light.
(John 12:35–36)

I have come as a light into the world, that whoever believes in Me should not abide in darkness.
(John 12:46)

The Life

I am the resurrection and the life. He who believes in Me, though he may die, he shall live. And whoever lives and believes in Me shall never die.
(John 11:25–26)

I am the way, the truth, and the life. No one comes to the Father except through Me.
(John 14:6)

His Authority

❧

[*To the disciples of John who asked if He was the Christ*]

Go and tell John the things which you hear and see:
The blind see and the lame walk; the lepers are
cleansed and the deaf hear; the dead are raised up
and the poor have the gospel preached to them.
And blessed is he who is not offended because of
Me.

(Matthew 11:4–6; cf. Luke 7:22–23)

(All things have been delivered to Me by My Father,
and no one knows the Son except the Father. Nor
does anyone know the Father except the Son, and
the one to whom the Son wills to reveal Him.

(Matthew 11:27; cf. Luke 10:22)

Every kingdom divided against itself is brought to
desolation, and every city or house divided against
itself will not stand. If Satan casts out Satan, he is
divided against himself. How then will his kingdom
stand? And if I cast out demons by Beelzebub, by
whom do your sons cast them out? Therefore they
shall be your judges. But if I cast out demons by the
Spirit of God, surely the kingdom of God has come

upon you. Or how can one enter a strong man's house and plunder his goods, unless he first binds the strong man? And then he will plunder his house.

(Matthew 12:25–29; cf. Mark 3:23–27, Luke 11:17–22)

Assuredly, I say to you, whatever you bind on earth will be bound in heaven, and whatever you loose on earth will be loosed in heaven. Again I say to you that if two of you agree on earth concerning anything that they ask, it will be done for them by My Father in heaven. For where two or three are gathered together in My name, I am there in the midst of them.

(Matthew 18:18–20)

Why do you reason about these things in your hearts? Which is easier, to say to the paralytic, "Your sins are forgiven you," or to say, "Arise, take up your bed and walk"? But that you may know that the Son of Man has power on earth to forgive sins I say to you, arise, take up your bed, and go to your house.

(Mark 2:8–11)

I can of Myself do nothing. As I hear, I judge; and My judgment is righteous, because I do not seek My own will but the will of the Father who sent Me. If I bear witness of Myself, My witness is not true. There is another who bears witness of Me, and I know that the witness which He witnesses of Me is true. You have sent to John, and he has borne witness to the truth. Yet I do not receive testimony from man, but I say these things that you might be saved. He was the burning and shining lamp, and you were willing for a time to rejoice in his light. But I have a greater witness than John's; for the works which the Father has given Me to finish—the very works that I do—bear witness of Me, that the Father has sent Me. And the Father Himself, who sent Me, has testified of Me. You have neither heard His voice at any time, nor seen His form. But you do not have His word abiding in you, because whom He sent, Him you do not believe.

(John 5:30–38)

My doctrine is not Mine, but His who sent Me. If anyone wills to do His will, He shall know concerning the doctrine, whether it is from God or whether I speak on my own authority. He who speaks from himself seeks his own glory; but He who seeks the glory of the One who sent Him is true, and no unrighteousness is in Him.

(John 7:16–18)

You both know Me, and you know where I am from; and I have not come of Myself, but He who sent Me is true, whom you do not know. But I know Him, for I am from Him, and He sent Me.

(John 7:28–29)

Even if I bear witness of Myself, My witness is true, for I know where I came from and where I am going; but you do not know where I come from and where I am going. You judge according to the flesh; I judge no one. And yet if I do judge, My judgment is true; for I am not alone, but I am with the Father who sent Me. It is also written in your law that the testimony of two men is true. I am One who bears witness of Myself, and the Father who sent Me bears witness of Me. You know neither Me nor My Father. If you had known Me, you would have known My Father also.

(John 8:14–19)

If God were your Father, you would love Me, for I proceeded forth and came from God; nor have I come of Myself, but He sent Me.

(John 8:42)

I told you, and you do not believe. The works that I do in My Father's name, they bear witness of Me.

(John 10:25)

Is it not written in your law, "I said, 'You are gods'"? If He called them gods, to whom the word of God came (and the Scripture cannot be broken), do you say of Him whom the Father sanctified and sent into the world, "You are blaspheming," because I said, "I am the Son of God"? If I do not do the works of My Father, do not believe Me; but if I do, though you do not believe Me, believe the works, that you may know and believe that the Father is in Me, and I in Him.

(John 10:34–38)

He who believes in Me, believes not in Me but in Him who sent Me. And he who sees Me sees Him who sent Me.

(John 12:44–45)

Most assuredly, I say to you, he who receives whomever I send receives Me; and he who receives Me receives Him who sent Me.

(John 13:20)

His Relationship to the Father

 za

Abba, Father, all things are possible for You. Take this cup away from Me; nevertheless, not what I will, but what You will.
(Mark 14:36; cf. Matt. 26:39, Luke 22:42)

"Most assuredly, I say to you, the Son can do nothing of Himself, but what He sees the Father do; for whatever He does, the Son also does in like manner. For the Father loves the Son, and shows Him all things that He Himself does; and He will show Him greater works than these, that you may marvel. For as the Father raises the dead and gives life to them, even so the Son gives life to whom He will. For the Father judges no one, but has committed all judgment to the Son, that all should honor the Son just as they honor the Father. He who does not honor the Son does not honor the Father who sent Him.
(John 5:19–23)

When you lift up the Son of Man, then you will know that I am He, and that I do nothing of Myself;

but as My Father taught Me, I speak these things. And He who sent Me is with Me. The Father has not left Me alone, for I always do those things that please Him.

(John 8:28–29)

If I honor Myself, My honor is nothing. It is My Father who honors Me, of whom you say that He is your God. Yet you have not known Him, but I know Him. And if I say, "I do not know Him," I shall be a liar like you; but I do know Him and keep His word.

(John 8:54–55)

I and My Father are one.

(John 10:30)

If you had known Me, you would have known My Father also; and from now on you know Him and have seen Him.

(John 14:7)

Have I been with you so long, and yet you have not known Me, Philip? He who has seen Me has seen the Father; so how can you say, "Show us the Father"? Do you not believe that I am in the Father, and the Father in Me? The words that I speak to you I do not speak on My own authority; but the Father who dwells in Me does the works. Believe Me that I am in the Father and the Father in Me, or else believe Me for the sake of the works themselves.

(John 14:9–11)

He who hates Me hates My Father also. If I had not done among them the works which no one else did, they would have no sin; but now they have seen and also hated both Me and My Father. But this happened that the word might be fulfilled which is written in their law, "They hated Me without a cause."

(John 15:23–25)

His Mission

 презент

Those who are well have no need of a physician,
but those who are sick. But go and learn what this
means: "I desire mercy and not sacrifice." For I did
not come to call the righteous, but sinners, to repentance.
(Matthew 9:12–13; cf. Mark 2:17, Luke 5:31–32)

I was not sent except to the lost sheep of the house
of Israel.
(Matthew 15:24)

Let us go into the next towns, that I may preach
there also, because for this purpose I have come
forth.
(Mark 1:38; cf. Luke 4:43)

[*Reading from Isaiah*]
"The Spirit of the Lord is upon Me, because He has
anointed Me to preach the gospel to the poor; He
has sent Me to heal the brokenhearted, to proclaim
liberty to the captives and recovery of sight to the
blind, to set at liberty those who are oppressed; to

proclaim the acceptable year of the Lord." Today this Scripture is fulfilled in your hearing.
(Luke 4:18–19, 21)

I came to send fire on the earth, and how I wish it were already kindled! But I have a baptism to be baptized with, and how distressed I am till it is accomplished! Do you suppose that I came to give peace on earth? I tell you, not at all, but rather division. For from now on five in one house will be divided: three against two, and two against three. Father will be divided against son and son against father, mother against daughter and daughter against mother, mother-in-law against her daughter-in-law and daughter-in-law against her mother-in-law.
(Luke 12:49–53; cf. Matthew 10:34–36, Mark 10:38)

What man of you, having a hundred sheep, if he loses one of them, does not leave the ninety-nine in the wilderness, and go after the one which is lost until he finds it? And when he has found it, he lays it on his shoulders, rejoicing. And when he comes home, he calls together his friends and neighbors, saying to them, "Rejoice with me, for I have found my sheep which was lost!" I say to you that likewise there will be more joy in heaven over one sinner who repents than over ninety-nine just persons who need no repentance.
(Luke 15:4–7; cf. Matthew 18:12–14)

Or what woman, having ten silver coins, if she loses one coin, does not light a lamp, sweep the house, and search carefully until she finds it? And when she has found it, she calls her friends and neighbors together, saying, "Rejoice with me, for I have found the piece which I lost!" Likewise, I say to you, there is joy in the presence of the angels of God over one sinner who repents.

(Luke 15:8–10)

[*Concerning Zacchaeus the publican*]

Today salvation has come to this house, because he also is a son of Abraham; for the Son of Man has come to seek and to save that which was lost.

(Luke 19:9–10)

My food is to do the will of Him who sent Me, and to finish His work.

(John 4:34)

My time has not yet come, but your time is always ready. The world cannot hate you, but it hates Me because I testify of it that its works are evil.

(John 7:6–7)

I have many things to say and to judge concerning you, but He who sent Me is true; and I speak to the world those things which I heard from Him.

(John 8:26)

For judgment I have come into this world, that those who do not see may see, and that those who see may be made blind.

(John 9:39)

The hour has come that the Son of Man should be glorified. Most assuredly, I say to you, unless a grain of wheat falls into the ground and dies, it remains alone; but if it dies, it produces much grain. He who loves his life will lose it, and he who hates his life in this world will keep it for eternal life. If anyone serves Me, let him follow Me; and where I am, there My servant will be also. If anyone serves Me, him My Father will honor. Now My soul is troubled, and what shall I say? "Father, save Me from this hour"? But for this purpose I came to this hour. Father, glorify Your name.

(John 12:23–28)

And if anyone hears My words and does not believe, I do not judge him; for I did not come to judge the world but to save the world. He who rejects Me, and does not receive My words, has that which judges him—the word that I have spoken will judge him in the last day. For I have not spoken on My own authority; but the Father who sent Me gave Me a command, what I should say and what I should speak. And I know that His command is everlasting life. Therefore, whatever I speak, just as the Father has told Me, so I speak.

(John 12:47–50)

If I had not come and spoken to them, they would have no sin, but now they have no excuse for their sin.

(John 15:22)

The Fulfillment
of Prophecy

❧

Put your sword in its place, for all who take the sword will perish by the sword. Or do you think that I cannot now pray to My Father, and He will provide Me with more than twelve legions of angels? How then could the Scriptures be fulfilled, that it must happen thus? Have you come out, as against a robber, with swords and clubs to take Me? I sat daily with you, teaching in the temple, and you did not seize Me. But all this was done that the Scriptures of the prophets might be fulfilled.

(Matthew 26:52–56; cf. Mark 14:48–49, Luke 22:52–53)

When I sent you without money bag, knapsack, and sandals, did you lack anything? But now, he who has a money bag, let him take it, and likewise a knapsack; and he who has no sword, let him sell his garment and buy one. For I say to you that this which is written must still be accomplished in Me: "And He was numbered with the transgressors." For the things concerning Me have an end.

(Luke 22:35–37)

O foolish ones, and slow of heart to believe in all that the prophets have spoken! Ought not the Christ to have suffered these things and to enter into His glory?

(Luke 24:25–26)

These are the words which I spoke to you while I was still with you, that all things must be fulfilled which were written in the Law of Moses and the Prophets and the Psalms concerning Me. Thus it is written, and thus it was necessary for the Christ to suffer and to rise from the dead the third day, and that repentance and remission of sins should be preached in His name to all nations, beginning at Jerusalem. And you are witnesses of these things.

(Luke 24:44, 46–48)

---·❧·---

TEACHINGS

---·❧·---

The Beatitudes

ε❧

Blessed are the poor in spirit, for theirs is the kingdom of heaven. Blessed are those who mourn, for they shall be comforted. Blessed are the meek, for they shall inherit the earth. Blessed are those who hunger and thirst for righteousness, for they shall be filled. Blessed are the merciful, for they shall obtain mercy. Blessed are the pure in heart, for they shall see God. Blessed are the peacemakers, for they shall be called sons of God. Blessed are those who are persecuted for righteousness' sake, for theirs is the kingdom of heaven. Blessed are you when they revile and persecute you, and say all kinds of evil against you falsely for My sake. Rejoice and be exceedingly glad, for great is your reward in heaven, for so they persecuted the prophets who were before you.

(Matthew 5:3–12; cf. Luke 6:20–23)

More than that, blessed are those who hear the word of God and keep it!

(Luke 11:28)

Warnings

ૐ

Woe to the world because of offenses! For offenses must come, but woe to that man by whom the offense comes!

(Matthew 18:7; cf. Luke 17:1)

But woe to you who are rich, for you have received your consolation. Woe to you who are full, for you shall hunger. Woe to you who laugh now, for you shall mourn and weep. Woe to you when all men speak well of you, for so did their fathers to the false prophets.

(Luke 6:24–26)

The New Birth

&

Most assuredly, I say to you, unless one is born again, he cannot see the kingdom of God.
(John 3:3)

Most assuredly, I say to you, unless one is born of water and the Spirit, he cannot enter the kingdom of God. That which is born of the flesh is flesh, and that which is born of the Spirit is spirit. Do not marvel that I said to you, "You must be born again." The wind blows where it wishes, and you hear the sound of it, but cannot tell where it comes from and where it goes. So is everyone who is born of the Spirit.
(John 3:5–8)

Eternal Life

❧

[*To a rich young ruler*]

Why do you call Me good? No one is good but One, that is, God. But if you want to enter into life, keep the commandments. "You shall not murder," "You shall not commit adultery," "You shall not steal," "You shall not bear false witness," "Honor your father and your mother," and "You shall love your neighbor as yourself." If you want to be perfect, go, sell what you have and give to the poor, and you will have treasure in heaven; and come, follow Me.
(Matthew 19:17–21; cf. Mark 10:18–21, Luke 18:19–22)

For God so loved the world that He gave His only begotten Son, that whoever believes in Him should not perish but have everlasting life. For God did not send His Son into the world to condemn the world, but that the world through Him might be saved. He who believes in Him is not condemned; but he who does not believe is condemned already, because he has not believed in the name of the only begotten Son of God. And this is the condemnation, that the light has come into the world, and men loved darkness rather than light, because their

deeds were evil. For everyone practicing evil hates the light and does not come to the light, lest his deeds should be exposed. But he who does the truth comes to the light, that his deeds may be clearly seen, that they have been done in God.
(John 3:16–21)

Most assuredly, I say to you, he who hears My word and believes in Him who sent Me has everlasting life, and shall not come into judgment, but has passed from death into life.
(John 5:24)

You search the Scriptures, for in them you think you have eternal life; and these are they which testify of Me. But you are not willing to come to Me that you may have life.
(John 5:39–40)

Do not labor for the food which perishes, but for the food which endures to everlasting life, which the Son of Man will give you, because God the Father has set His seal on Him.
(John 6:27)

And this is the will of Him who sent Me, that everyone who sees the Son and believes in Him may have everlasting life; and I will raise him up at the last day.
(John 6:40)

Most assuredly, I say to you, he who believes in Me
has everlasting life.
(John 6:47)

Whoever eats My flesh and drinks My blood has
eternal life, and I will raise him up at the last day.
(John 6:54)

Most assuredly, I say to you, if anyone keeps My
word he shall never see death.
(John 8:51)

The Pre-eminence of God

It is written, "Man shall not live by bread alone, but by every word that proceeds from the mouth of God."

(Matthew 4:4; cf. Luke 4:4)

It is written again, "You shall not tempt the Lord your God."

(Matthew 4:7; cf. Luke 4:12)

For it is written, "You shall worship the Lord your God, and Him only you shall serve."

(Matthew 4:10; cf. Luke 4:8)

Martha, Martha, you are worried and troubled about many things. But one thing is needed, and Mary has chosen that good part, which will not be taken away from her.

(Luke 10:41–42)

[*To Pilate*]

You could have no power at all against Me unless it had been given you from above. Therefore the one who delivered Me to you has the greater sin.

(John 19:11)

Deeds Rewarded

He who receives you receives Me, and he who receives Me receives Him who sent Me. He who receives a prophet in the name of a prophet shall receive a prophet's reward. And he who receives a righteous man in the name of a righteous man shall receive a righteous man's reward. And whoever gives one of these little ones only a cup of cold water in the name of a disciple, assuredly, I say to you, he shall by no means lose his reward.

(Matthew 10:40–42; cf. Mark 9:41, Luke 10:16)

When the Son of Man comes in His glory, and all the holy angels with Him, then He will sit on the throne of His glory. All the nations will be gathered before Him, and He will separate them one from another, as a shepherd divides his sheep from the goats. And He will set the sheep on His right hand, but the goats on His left. Then the King will say to those on His right hand, "Come, you blessed of My Father, inherit the kingdom prepared for you from the foundation of the world: for I was hungry and you gave Me food; I was thirsty and you gave Me drink; I was a stranger and you took Me in; I was naked and you clothed Me; I was sick and you visited Me; I was in prison and you came to Me." Then the righteous will answer Him, saying, "Lord, when did we see You hungry and feed You, or thirsty and give You drink? When did we see You a stranger and take You in, or naked and clothe You? Or when did we see You sick, or in prison, and come to You?" And the King will answer and say to them, "Assuredly, I say to you, inasmuch as you did it to one of the least of these My brethren, you did it to Me." Then He will also say to those on the left hand, "Depart from Me, you cursed, into the everlasting fire prepared for the devil and his angels: for I was hungry and you gave Me no food; I was thirsty and you gave Me no drink; I was a stranger and you did not take Me in, naked and you did not clothe Me, sick and in prison and you did not visit Me." Then they also will answer Him, saying, "Lord, when did we see You hungry or thirsty or a stranger or naked or sick or in prison, and did not minister to you?" Then He will answer them, saying, "Assuredly, I say to you, inasmuch as you did not do it to one of the least of these, you did not do it to Me." And these will go away into everlasting punishment, but the righteous into eternal life.

(Matthew 25:31–46)

When you give a dinner or a supper, do not ask your friends, your brothers, your relatives, nor rich neighbors, lest they also invite you back, and you be repaid. But when you give a feast, invite the poor, the maimed, the lame, the blind. And you will be blessed, because they cannot repay you; for you shall be repaid at the resurrection of the just.

(Luke 14:12–14)

The Importance of Guarding
One's Speech

৶

But I say to you that for every idle word men may speak, they will give account of it in the day of judgment. For by your words you will be justified, and by your words you will be condemned.

(Matthew 12:36–37)

Not what goes into the mouth defiles a man; but what comes out of the mouth, this defiles a man.

(Matthew 15:11; cf. Mark 7:15)

Do you not yet understand that whatever enters the mouth goes into the stomach and is eliminated? But those things which proceed out of the mouth come from the heart, and they defile a man. For out of the heart proceed evil thoughts, murders, adulteries, fornications, thefts, false witness, blasphemies. These are the things which defile a man, but to eat with unwashed hands does not defile a man.

(Matthew 15:17–20; cf. Mark 7:18–23)

Children

❧

Whoever receives one little child like this in My name receives Me. But whoever causes one of these little ones who believe in Me to sin, it would be better for him if a millstone were hung around his neck, and he were drowned in the depth of the sea.
(Matthew 18:5–6; cf. Mark 9:37, 42, Luke 9:48, 17:2)

Take heed that you do not despise one of these little ones, for I say to you that in heaven their angels always see the face of My Father who is in heaven.
(Matthew 18:10)

Even so it is not the will of your Father who is in heaven that one of these little ones should perish.
(Matthew 18:14)

Let the little children come to Me, and do not forbid them; for of such is the kingdom of heaven.
(Matthew 19:14; cf. Mark 10:14, Luke 18:16)

Yes. Have you never read, "Out of the mouth of babes and nursing infants You have perfected praise"?
(Matthew 21:16)

It is impossible that no offenses should come, but woe to him through whom they do come! It would be better for him if a millstone were hung around his neck, and he were thrown into the sea, than that he should offend one of these little ones.

(Luke 17:1–2; cf. Matthew 18:6–7, Mark 9:42)

Marriage and Divorce

ૐ

Furthermore it has been said, "Whoever divorces his wife, let him give her a certificate of divorce." But I say to you that whoever divorces his wife for any reason except sexual immorality causes her to commit adultery; and whoever marries a woman who is divorced commits adultery.

(Matthew 5:31–32; cf. Luke 16:18)

Have you not read that He who made them at the beginning "made them male and female," and said, "For this reason a man shall leave his father and mother and be joined to his wife, and the two shall become one flesh"? So then, they are no longer two but one flesh. Therefore what God has joined together, let not man separate.

(Matthew 19:4–6)

Moses, because of the hardness of your hearts, permitted you to divorce your wives, but from the beginning it was not so. And I say to you, whoever divorces his wife, except for sexual immorality, and

marries another, commits adultery; and whoever marries her who is divorced commits adultery.
(Matthew 19:8–9)

[*In response to the suggestion that people shouldn't marry*]

All cannot accept this saying, but only those to whom it has been given: for there are eunuchs who were born thus from their mother's womb, and there are eunuchs who were made eunuchs by men, and there are eunuchs who have made themselves eunuchs for the kingdom of heaven's sake. He who is able to accept it, let him accept it.
(Matthew 19:11–12)

Riches

Do not lay up for yourselves treasures on earth, where moth and rust destroy and where thieves break in and steal; but lay up for yourselves treasures in heaven, where neither moth nor rust destroys and where thieves do not break in and steal. For where your treasure is, there your heart will be also. The lamp of the body is the eye. If therefore your eye is good, your whole body will be full of light. But if your eye is bad, your whole body will be full of darkness. If therefore the light that is in you is darkness, how great is that darkness! No one can serve two masters; for either he will hate the one and love the other, or else he will be loyal to the one and despise the other. You cannot serve God and mammon.

(Matthew 6:19–24; cf. Luke 12:33–35, 16:13)

Assuredly, I say to you that it is hard for a rich man to enter the kingdom of heaven. And again I say to you, it is easier for a camel to go through the eye of a needle than for a rich man to enter the kingdom of God. With men this is impossible, but with God all things are possible.

(Matthew 19:23–24, 26; cf. Mark 10:24–27, Luke 18:24–27)

[*Upon being asked to divide an inheritance*]

Man, who made Me a judge or an arbitrator over you? Take heed and beware of covetousness, for one's life does not consist in the abundance of the things he possesses.

(Luke 12:14–15)

Bearing Fruit

Beware of false prophets, who come to you in sheep's clothing, but inwardly they are ravenous wolves. You will know them by their fruits. Do men gather grapes from thornbushes or figs from thistles? Even so, every good tree bears good fruit, but a bad tree bears bad fruit. A good tree cannot bear bad fruit, nor can a bad tree bear good fruit. Every tree that does not bear good fruit is cut down and thrown into the fire. Therefore by their fruits you will know them.

(Matthew 7:15–20; cf. Luke 6:43–44)

Either make the tree good and its fruit good, or else make the tree bad and its fruit bad; for a tree is known by its fruit. Brood of vipers! How can you, being evil, speak good things? For out of the abundance of the heart the mouth speaks. A good man out of the good treasure of his heart brings forth good things, and an evil man out of the evil treasure brings forth evil things.

(Matthew 12:33–35; cf. Luke 6:45)

I am the true vine, and My Father is the vinedresser. Every branch in Me that does not bear fruit He takes away; and every branch that bears fruit He prunes, that it may bear more fruit. You are already clean because of the word which I have spoken to you. Abide in Me, and I in you. As the branch cannot bear fruit of itself, unless it abides in the vine, neither can you, unless you abide in Me. I am the vine, you are the branches. He who abides in Me, and I in him, bears much fruit; for without Me you can do nothing. If anyone does not abide in Me, he is cast out as a branch and is withered; and they gather them and throw them into the fire, and they are burned. If you abide in Me, and My words abide in you, you will ask what you desire, and it shall be done for you. By this My Father is glorified, that you bear much fruit; so you will be My disciples.

(John 15:1–8)

Taxes and Tribute

&

What do you think, Simon? From whom do the kings of the earth take customs or taxes, from their sons or from strangers? [*Peter answered, "From strangers."*] Then the sons are free. Nevertheless, lest we offend them, go to the sea, cast in a hook, and take the fish that comes up first. And when you have opened its mouth, you will find a piece of money; take that and give it to them for Me and you.
(Matthew 17:25–27)

Render therefore to Caesar the things that are Caesar's, and to God the things that are God's.
(Matthew 22:21; cf. Mark 12:15–17, Luke 20:24–25)

Hell

ૐ

But the sons of the kingdom will be cast out into outer darkness. There will be weeping and gnashing of teeth.

(Matthew 8:12; cf. Matthew 13:42, 13:50, 22:13, 24:51, 25:30)

And do not fear those who kill the body but cannot kill the soul. But rather fear Him who is able to destroy both soul and body in hell.

(Matthew 10:28; cf. Luke 12:4, 5)

Then He will also say to those on the left hand, "Depart from Me, you cursed, into the everlasting fire prepared for the devil and his angels. . . . And these will go away into everlasting punishment, but the righteous into eternal life.

(Matthew 25:41, 46)

Thoughts and Behavior

❧

You have heard that it was said to those of old, "You shall not murder, and whoever murders will be in danger of the judgment." But I say to you that whoever is angry with his brother without a cause shall be in danger of the judgment. And whoever says to his brother, "Raca!" shall be in danger of the council. But whoever says, "You fool!" shall be in danger of hell fire. Therefore if you bring your gift to the altar, and there remember that your brother has something against you, leave your gift there before the altar, and go your way. First be reconciled to your brother, and then come and offer your gift. Agree with your adversary quickly, while you are on the way with him, lest your adversary deliver you to the judge, the judge hand you over to the officer, and you be thrown into prison. Assuredly, I say to you, you will by no means get out of there till you have paid the last penny.

(Matthew 5:21–26; cf. Luke 12:58–59)

You have heard that it was said to those of old, "You shall not commit adultery." But I say to you that whoever looks at a woman to lust for her has already committed adultery with her in his heart. If your right eye causes you to sin, pluck it out and cast it from you; for it is more profitable for you that one of your members perish, than for your whole body to be cast into hell. And if your right hand causes you to sin, cut it off and cast it from you; for it is more profitable for you that one of your members perish, than for your whole body to be cast into hell.

(Matthew 5:27–30; cf. Mark 9:43, 47)

Again you have heard that it was said to those of old, "You shall not swear falsely, but shall perform your oaths to the Lord." But I say to you, do not swear at all: neither by heaven, for it is God's throne; nor by the earth, for it is His footstool; nor by Jerusalem, for it is the city of the great King. Nor shall you swear by your head, because you cannot make one hair white or black. But let your "Yes" be "Yes," and your "No," "No." For whatever is more than these is from the evil one.

(Matthew 5:33–37)

Therefore you shall be perfect, just as your Father in heaven is perfect.

(Matthew 5:48)

Commitment

&

You are the salt of the earth; but if the salt loses its flavor, how shall it be seasoned? It is then good for nothing but to be thrown out and trampled underfoot by men. You are the light of the world. A city that is set on a hill cannot be hidden. Nor do they light a lamp and put it under a basket, but on a lampstand, and it gives light to all who are in the house. Let your light so shine before men, that they may see your good works and glorify your Father in heaven.

(Matthew 5:13–16; cf. Mark 4:21, 9:50, Luke 8:16; 11:33)

If your hand causes you to sin, cut it off. It is better for you to enter into life maimed, rather than having two hands, to go to hell, into the fire that shall never be quenched—where "Their worm does not die and the fire is not quenched." And if your foot causes you to sin, cut it off. It is better for you to enter life lame, rather than having two feet, to be cast into hell, into the fire that shall never be quenched—where "Their worm does not die and the fire is not quenched." And if your eye causes you to sin, pluck it out. It is better for you to enter the kingdom of God with one eye, rather than having two eyes, to be cast into hell fire—where "Their worm does not die and the fire is not quenched." For everyone will be seasoned with fire, and every sacrifice will be seasoned with salt.

(Mark 9:43–49; cf. Matthew 18:8–9)

If anyone comes to Me and does not hate his father and mother, wife and children, brothers and sisters, yes, and his own life also, he cannot be My disciple. And whoever does not bear his cross and come after Me cannot be My disciple. For which of you, intending to build a tower, does not sit down first and count the cost, whether he has enough to finish it—lest, after he has laid the foundation, and is not able to finish it, all who see it begin to mock him, saying, "This man began to build and was not able to finish." Or what king, going to make war against another king, does not sit down first and consider whether he is able with ten thousand to meet him who comes against him with twenty thousand? Or else, while the other is still a great way off, he sends a delegation and asks conditions of peace. So likewise, whoever of you does not forsake all that he has cannot be My disciple. Salt is good; but if the salt has lost its flavor, how shall it be seasoned? It is neither fit for the land nor for the dunghill, but men throw it out. He who has ears to hear, let him hear!

(Luke 14:26–35; cf. Matthew 5:13, 10:37–38, Mark 9:50)

Submission

è.

You have heard that it was said, "An eye for an eye and a tooth for a tooth." But I tell you not to resist an evil person. But whoever slaps you on your right cheek, turn the other to him also. If anyone wants to sue you and take away your tunic, let him have your cloak also. And whoever compels you to go one mile, go with him two. Give to him who asks you, and from him who wants to borrow from you do not turn away.

(Matthew 5:38–42; cf. Luke 6:29–30)

But you, do not be called "Rabbi"; for One is your Teacher, the Christ, and you are all brethren. Do not call anyone on earth your father; for One is your Father, He who is in heaven. And do not be called teachers; for One is your Teacher, the Christ. But he who is greatest among you shall be your servant. And whoever exalts himself will be humbled, and he who humbles himself will be exalted.

(Matthew 23:8–12; cf. Mark 9:35)

When you are invited by anyone to a wedding feast, do not sit down in the best place, lest one more honorable than you be invited by him; and he who invited you and him come and say to you, "Give place to this man," and then you begin with shame to take the lowest place. But when you are invited, go and sit down in the lowest place, so that when he who invited you comes he may say to you, "Friend, go up higher." Then you will have glory in the presence of those who sit at the table with you. For whoever exalts himself will be humbled, and he who humbles himself will be exalted.

(Luke 14:8–11; cf. Matthew 23:12)

And which of you, having a servant plowing or tending sheep, will say to him when he has come in from the field, "Come at once and sit down to eat"? But will he not rather say to him, "Prepare something for my supper, and gird yourself and serve me till I have eaten and drunk, and afterward you will eat and drink"? Does he thank that servant because he did the things that were commanded him? I think not. So likewise you, when you have done all those things which you are commanded, say, "We are unprofitable servants. We have done what was our duty to do."

(Luke 17:7–10)

You call Me Teacher and Lord, and you say well, for so I am. If I then, your Lord and Teacher, have washed your feet, you also ought to wash one another's feet. For I have given you an example, that you should do as I have done to you. Most assuredly, I say to you, a servant is not greater than his master; nor is he who is sent greater than he who sent him. If you know these things, blessed are you if you do them.

(John 13:13–17)

Trust

è.

Therefore I say to you, do not worry about your life, what you will eat or what you will drink; nor about your body, what you will put on. Is not life more than food and the body more than clothing? Look at the birds of the air, for they neither sow nor reap nor gather into barns; yet your heavenly Father feeds them. Are you not of more value than they? Which of you by worrying can add one cubit to his stature? So why do you worry about clothing? Consider the lilies of the field, how they grow: they neither toil nor spin; and yet I say to you that even Solomon in all his glory was not arrayed like one of these. Now if God so clothes the grass of the field, which today is, and tomorrow is thrown into the oven, will He not much more clothe you, O you of little faith? Therefore do not worry, saying, "What shall we eat?" or "What shall we drink?" or "What shall we wear?" For after all these the Gentiles seek. For your heavenly Father knows that you need all these things. But seek first the kingdom of God and His righteousness, and all these things shall be added to you. Therefore do not worry about tomorrow, for tomorrow will worry about its own things. Sufficient for the day is its own trouble. (Matthew 6:25–34; cf. Luke 12:22–31)

Worship

Woman, believe Me, the hour is coming when you
will neither on this mountain, nor in Jerusalem,
worship the Father. You worship what you do not
know; we know what we worship, for salvation is
of the Jews. But the hour is coming, and now is,
when the true worshippers will worship the Father
in spirit and truth; for the Father is seeking such to
worship Him. God is Spirit, and those who worship
Him must worship in spirit and truth.

(John 4:21–24)

Religious Practices

Take heed that you do not do your charitable deeds before men, to be seen by them. Otherwise you have no reward from your Father in heaven. Therefore, when you do a charitable deed, do not sound a trumpet before you as the hypocrites do in the synagogues and in the streets, that they may have glory from men. Assuredly, I say to you, they have their reward. But when you do a charitable deed, do not let your left hand know what your right hand is doing, that your charitable deed may be in secret; and your Father who sees in secret will Himself reward you openly.

(Matthew 6:1–4)

Moreover, when you fast, do not be like the hypocrites, with a sad countenance. For they disfigure their faces that they may appear to men to be fasting. Assuredly, I say to you, they have their reward. But you, when you fast, anoint your head and wash your face, so that you do not appear to men to be fasting, but to your Father who is in the secret place; and your Father who sees in secret will reward you openly.

(Matthew 6:16–18)

Do not give what is holy to the dogs; nor cast your pearls before swine, lest they trample them under their feet, and turn and tear you in pieces.

(Matthew 7:6)

Faith

Go your way; and as you have believed, so let it be done for you.
(Matthew 8:13)

Be of good cheer, daughter, your faith has made you well.
(Matthew 9:22; cf. Mark 5:34, Luke 8:48)

According to your faith let it be to you.
(Matthew 9:29)

O woman, great is your faith! Let it be to you as you desire.
(Matthew 15:28; cf. Mark 7:29)

Assuredly, I say to you, if you have faith as a mustard seed, you will say to this mountain, "Move from here to there," and it will move; and nothing will be impossible for you.
(Matthew 17:20; cf. Luke 17:6)

Assuredly, I say to you, if you have faith and do not doubt, you will not only do what was done to the

fig tree, but also if you say to this mountain, "Be removed and be cast into the sea," it will be done. And whatever things you ask in prayer, believing, you will receive.
(Matthew 21:21–22; cf. Mark 11:22–23, Luke 17:6)

Do not be afraid; only believe.
(Mark 5:36; cf. Luke 8:50)

If you can believe, all things are possible to him who believes.
(Mark 9:23)

I say to you, I have not found such great faith, not even in Israel!
(Luke 7:9)

Your sins are forgiven. Your faith has saved you. Go in Peace.
(Luke 7:48, 50)

Do not be afraid; only believe, and she will be made well!
(Luke 8:50; cf. Mark 5:36)

Which of you shall have a friend, and go to him at midnight and say to him, "Friend, lend me three loaves; for a friend of mine has come to me on his journey, and I have nothing to set before him"; and he will answer from within and say, "Do not trou-

ble me; the door is now shut, and my children are with me in bed; I cannot rise and give to you"? I say to you, though he will not rise and give to him because he is his friend, yet because of his persistence he will rise and give him as many as he needs. So I say to you, ask, and it will be given to you; seek, and you will find; knock, and it will be opened to you. For everyone who asks receives, and he who seeks finds, and to him who knocks it will be opened. If a son asks for bread from any father among you, will he give him a stone? Or if he asks for a fish, will he give him a serpent instead of a fish? Or if he asks for an egg, will he offer him a scorpion? If you then, being evil, know how to give good gifts to your children, how much more will your heavenly Father give the Holy Spirit to those who ask Him!
(Luke 11:5–13; cf. Matthew 7:7–11)

[*To the one leper, of ten, who came back to give thanks*]

Were there not ten cleansed? But where are the nine? Were there not any found who returned to give glory to God except this foreigner? Arise, go your way. Your faith has made you well.
(Luke 17:17–19)

Why are you troubled? And why do doubts arise in your hearts? Behold My hands and My feet, that it is I Myself. Handle Me and see, for a spirit does not have flesh and bones as you see I have.
(Luke 24:38–39)

This is the work of God, that you believe in Him whom He sent.

(John 6:29)

Most assuredly, I say to you, he who believes in Me, the works that I do he will do also; and greater works than these he will do, because I go to My Father. And whatever you ask in My name, that I will do, that the Father may be glorified in the Son. If you ask anything in My name, I will do it.

(John 14:12–14)

Reach your finger here, and look at My hands; and reach your hand here, and put it into My side. Do not be unbelieving, but believing.

(John 20:27)

Love and Obedience

❧

You have heard that it was said, "You shall love your neighbor and hate your enemy." But I say to you, love your enemies, bless those who curse you, do good to those who hate you, and pray for those who spitefully use you and persecute you, that you may be sons of your Father in heaven; for He makes His sun rise on the evil and on the good, and sends rain on the just and on the unjust.

(Matthew 5:43–45)

"You shall love the Lord your God with all your heart, with all your soul, and with all your mind." This is the first and great commandment. And the second is like it: "You shall love your neighbor as yourself." On these two commandments hang all the Law and the Prophets.

(Matthew 22:37–40; cf. Mark 12:29–31, Luke 10:27)

But I say to you who hear: Love your enemies, do good to those who hate you, bless those who curse you, and pray for those who spitefully use you.

(Luke 6:27–28)

But if you love those who love you, what credit is that to you? For even sinners love those who love them. And if you do good to those who do good to you, what credit is that to you? For even sinners do the same. And if you lend to those from whom you hope to receive back, what credit is that to you? For even sinners lend to sinners to receive as much back. But love your enemies, do good, and lend, hoping for nothing in return; and your reward will be great, and you will be sons of the Most High. For He is kind to the unthankful and evil. Therefore be merciful, just as your Father also is merciful.

(Luke 6:32–36; cf. Matthew 5:46–48)

A new commandment I give to you, that you love one another; as I have loved you, that you also love one another. By this all will know that you are My disciples, if you have love for one another.

(John 13:34–35)

If you love Me, keep My commandments.

(John 14:15)

He who has My commandments and keeps them, it is he who loves Me. And he who loves Me will be loved by My Father, and I will love him and manifest Myself to him.

(John 14:21)

If anyone loves Me, he will keep My word; and My Father will love him, and We will come to him and make Our home with him. He who does not love Me does not keep My words; and the word which you hear is not Mine but the Father's who sent Me.
(John 14:23–24)

This is My commandment, that you love one another as I have loved you.
(John 15:12)

These things I command you, that you love one another.
(John 15:17)

Reproof and Forgiveness

Judge not, that you be not judged. For with what judgment you judge, you will be judged; and with the measure you use, it will be measured back to you. And why do you look at the speck in your brother's eye, but do not consider the plank in your own eye? Or how can you say to your brother, "Let me remove the speck from your eye"; and look, a plank is in your own eye? Hypocrite! First remove the plank from your own eye, and then you will see clearly to remove the speck from your brother's eye.

(Matthew 7:1–5; cf. Mark 4:24, Luke 6:37–38)

Moreover if your brother sins against you, go and tell him his fault between you and him alone. If he hears you, you have gained your brother. But if he will not hear, take with you one or two more, that "by the mouth of two or three witnesses every word may be established." And if he refuses to hear them, tell it to the church. But if he refuses even to hear the church, let him be to you like a heathen and a tax collector.

(Matthew 18:15–17; cf. Luke 17:3)

[*When Peter asked if he should forgive his brother seven times*]

I do not say to you, up to seven times, but up to seventy times seven.

(Matthew 18:22; cf. Luke 17:4)

And whenever you stand praying, if you have anything against anyone, forgive him, that your Father in heaven may also forgive you your trespasses. But if you do not forgive, neither will your Father in heaven forgive your trespasses.

(Mark 11:25–26; cf. Matthew 6:14–15, 18:35)

He who is without sin among you, let him throw a stone at her first.

(John 8:7; see also parables on forgiveness)

Giving

આ

Give, and it will be given to you: good measure, pressed down, shaken together, and running over will be put into your bosom. For with the same measure that you use, it will be measured back to you.

(Luke 6:38)

[Upon seeing a poor widow donate two small copper coins]

Truly I say to you that this poor widow has put in more than all; for all these out of their abundance have put in offerings for God, but she out of her poverty put in all the livelihood that she had.

(Luke 21:3–4; cf. Mark 12:43–44)

The Proper Role
of the Law

❧

Do not think that I came to destroy the Law or the Prophets. I did not come to destroy but to fulfill. For assuredly, I say to you, till heaven and earth pass away, one jot or one tittle will by no means pass from the law till all is fulfilled. Whoever therefore breaks one of the least of these commandments, and teaches men so, shall be called least in the kingdom of heaven; but whoever does and teaches them, he shall be called great in the kingdom of heaven. For I say to you, that unless your righteousness exceeds the righteousness of the scribes and Pharisees, you will by no means enter the kingdom of heaven.

(Matthew 5:17–20; cf. Luke 16:17)

Therefore, whatever you want men to do to you, do also to them, for this is the Law and the Prophets.

(Matthew 7:12; cf. Luke 6:31)

Have you not read what David did when he was hungry, he and those who were with him: how he entered the house of God and ate the showbread which was not lawful for him to eat, nor for those who were with him, but only for the priests? Or have you not read in the law that on the Sabbath the priests in the temple profane the Sabbath, and are blameless? Yet I say to you that in this place there is One greater than the temple. But if you had known what this means, "I desire mercy and not sacrifice," you would not have condemned the guiltless. For the Son of Man is Lord even of the Sabbath.

(Matthew 12:3–8; cf. Mark 2:25–28, Luke 6:3–5)

What man is there among you who has one sheep, and if it falls into a pit on the Sabbath, will not lay hold of it and lift it out? Of how much more value then is a man than a sheep? Therefore it is lawful to do good on the Sabbath.

(Matthew 12:11–12; cf. Mark 3:4, Luke 6:9, 14:5)

I did one work, and you all marvel. Moses therefore gave you circumcision (not that it is from Moses, but from the fathers), and you circumcise a man on the Sabbath. If a man receives circumcision on the Sabbath, so that the law of Moses should not be broken, are you angry with Me because I made a man completely well on the Sabbath? Do not judge according to appearance, but judge with righteous judgment.

(John 7:21–24)

The Holy Spirit

Therefore I say to you, every sin and blasphemy will be forgiven men, but the blasphemy against the Spirit will not be forgiven men. Anyone who speaks a word against the Son of Man, it will be forgiven him; but whoever speaks against the Holy Spirit, it will not be forgiven him, either in this age or in the age to come.

(Matthew 12:31–32; cf. Mark 3:28–29, Luke 12:10)

It is the Spirit who gives life; the flesh profits nothing. The words that I speak to you are spirit, and they are life.

(John 6:63)

Evil Spirits

When an unclean spirit goes out of a man, he goes through dry places, seeking rest, and finds none. Then he says, "I will return to my house from which I came." And when he comes, he finds it empty, swept, and put in order. Then he goes and takes with him seven other spirits more wicked than himself, and they enter and dwell there; and the last state of that man is worse than the first. So shall it also be with this wicked generation.

(Matthew 12:43–45; cf. Luke 11:24–26)

This kind [*of spirit*] can come out by nothing but prayer and fasting.

(Mark 9:29)

Warning Against Signs

An evil and adulterous generation seeks after a sign, and no sign will be given to it except the sign of the prophet Jonah. For as Jonah was three days and three nights in the belly of the great fish, so will the Son of Man be three days and three nights in the heart of the earth. The men of Ninevah will rise up in the judgment with this generation and condemn it, because they repented at the preaching of Jonah; and indeed a greater than Jonah is here. The queen of the South will rise up in the judgment with this generation and condemn it, for she came from the ends of the earth to hear the wisdom of Solomon; and indeed a greater than Solomon is here.

(Matthew 12:39–42; cf. Luke 11:29–31)

When it is evening you say, "It will be fair weather, for the sky is red"; and in the morning, "It will be foul weather today, for the sky is red and threatening." Hypocrites! You know how to discern the face of the sky, but you cannot discern the signs of the times. A wicked and adulterous generation seeks after a sign, and no sign shall be given to it except the sign of the prophet Jonah.

(Matthew 16:2–4; cf. Mark 8:12, Luke 11:29, 12:54–56)

For false christs and false prophets will rise and show great signs and wonders to deceive, if possible, even the elect.

(Matthew 24:24)

Unless you people see signs and wonders, you will by no means believe.

(John 4:48)

Thomas, because you have seen Me, you have believed. Blessed are those who have not seen and yet have believed.

(John 20:29)

The Kingdom of God

Entering the Kingdom

Enter by the narrow gate; for wide is the gate and broad is the way that leads to destruction, and there are many who go in by it. Because narrow is the gate and difficult is the way which leads to life, and there are few who find it.

(Matthew 7:13–14; cf. Luke 13:24)

Not everyone who says to Me, "Lord, Lord," shall enter the kingdom of heaven, but he who does the will of My Father in heaven. Many will say to Me in that day, "Lord, Lord, have we not prophesied in Your name, cast out demons in Your name, and done many wonders in Your name?" And I will declare to them, "I never knew you; depart from Me, you who practice lawlessness!"

(Matthew 7:21–23; cf. Luke 6:46, 13:27)

Therefore whoever confesses Me before men, him I will also confess before My Father who is in heaven. But whoever denies Me before men, him I will also deny before My Father who is in heaven.

(Matthew 10:32–33; cf. Luke 12:8–9)

If anyone desires to come after Me, let him deny himself, and take up his cross, and follow Me. For whoever desires to save his life will lose it, but whoever loses his life for My sake will find it. For what profit is it to a man if he gains the whole world, and loses his own soul? Or what will a man give in exchange for his soul?

(Matthew 16:24–26; cf. Mark 8:34–37, Luke 9:23–25)

For whoever is ashamed of Me and My words, of him the Son of Man will be ashamed when He comes in His own glory, and in His Father's, and of the holy angels.

(Luke 9:26; cf. Mark 8:38)

Strive to enter through the narrow gate, for many, I say to you, will seek to enter and will not be able. When once the Master of the house has risen up and shut the door, and you begin to stand outside and knock at the door, saying, "Lord, Lord, open for us," and He will answer and say to you, "I do not know you, where you are from," then you will begin to say, "We ate and drank in Your presence, and You taught in our streets." But He will say, "I tell you I do not know you, where you are from. Depart from Me, all you workers of iniquity." There will be weeping and gnashing of teeth, when you see Abraham and Isaac and Jacob and all the prophets in the kingdom of God, and yourselves thrust out. They will come from the east and the west, from the

north and the south, and sit down in the kingdom
of God. And indeed there are last who will be first,
and there are first who will be last.

(Luke 13:24–30; cf. Matthew 7–8, 19, 25)

The kingdom of God does not come with observa-
tion; nor will they say, "See here!" or "See there!"
For indeed, the kingdom of God is within you.

(Luke 17:20–21)

Therefore I have said to you that no one can come
to Me unless it has been granted to him by My
Father.

(John 6:65)

If you abide in My word, you are My disciples indeed. And you shall know the truth, and the truth
shall make you free.

(John 8:31–32)

Most assuredly, I say to you, whoever commits sin is
a slave of sin. And a slave does not abide in the
house forever, but a son abides forever. Therefore if
the Son makes you free, you shall be free indeed.

(John 8:34–36)

Position in the Kingdom

My kingdom is not of this world. If My kingdom
were of this world, My servants would fight, so that

I should not be delivered to the Jews; but now My kingdom is not from here.

(John 18:36–37)

Assuredly, I say to you, among those born of women there has not risen one greater than John the Baptist; but he who is least in the kingdom of heaven is greater than he.

(Matthew 11:11)

Assuredly, I say to you, unless you are converted and become as little children, you will by no means enter the kingdom of heaven. Therefore whoever humbles himself as this little child is the greatest in the kingdom of heaven.

(Matthew 18:3–4; cf. Mark 10:15, Luke 18:17)

Assuredly I say to you, that in the regeneration, when the Son of Man sits on the throne of His glory, you who have followed Me will also sit on twelve thrones, judging the twelve tribes of Israel. And everyone who has left houses or brothers or sisters or father or mother or wife or children or lands, for My name's sake, shall receive a hundredfold, and inherit eternal life. But many who are first will be last, and the last first.

(Matthew 19:28–30; cf. Mark 10:29–31, Luke 18:29–30, 22:30)

You will indeed drink My cup, and be baptized
with the baptism that I am baptized with; but to sit
on My right hand and on My left is not Mine to give,
but it is for those for whom it is prepared by My
Father.
(Matthew 20:23; cf. Mark 10:39–40, Luke 12:50)

You know that the rulers of the Gentiles lord it over
them, and those who are great exercise authority
over them. Yet it shall not be so among you; but
whoever desires to become great among you, let
him be your servant. And whoever desires to be
first among you, let him be your slave—just as the
Son of Man did not come to be served, but to serve,
and to give His life a ransom for many.
(Matthew 20:25–28; Mark 10:42–45, Luke 22:25–27)

Who is My mother, or My brothers? Here are My
mother and My brothers! For whoever does the
will of God is My brother and My sister and mother.
(Mark 3:33–35; cf. Matthew 12:48–50, Luke 8:21)

Do not forbid him, for no one who works a miracle
in My name can soon afterward speak evil of Me.
For he who is not against us is on our side.
(Mark 9:39–40; Matthew 12:30, Luke 9:50, 11:23)

Perceiving the Kingdom

[*When His disciples asked why he spoke in parables*]

Because it has been given to you to know the mysteries of the kingdom of heaven, but to them it has not been given. For whoever has, to him more will be given, and he will have abundance; but whoever does not have, even what he has will be taken away from him. Therefore I speak to them in parables, because seeing they do not see, and hearing they do not hear, nor do they understand. And in them the prophecy of Isaiah is fulfilled, which says: "Hearing you will hear and shall not understand, and seeing you will see and not perceive; for the hearts of this people have grown dull. Their ears are hard of hearing, and their eyes they have closed, lest they should see with their eyes and hear with their ears, lest they should understand with their hearts and turn, so that I should heal them." But blessed are your eyes for they see, and your ears for they hear; for assuredly, I say to you that many prophets and righteous men desired to see what you see, and did not see it, and to hear what you hear, and did not hear it.

(Matthew 13:11–17; cf. Mark 4:11–12, 4:25, Luke 8:10, 18, 24)

PROMISES TO HIS
FOLLOWERS

Authority

❧

[*When Peter said Jesus was the Christ*]

Blessed are you, Simon Bar-Jonah, for flesh and blood has not revealed this to you, but My Father who is in heaven. And I also say to you that you are Peter, and on this rock I will build My church, and the gates of Hades shall not prevail against it. And I will give you the keys of the kingdom of heaven, and whatever you bind on earth will be bound in heaven, and whatever you loose on earth will be loosed in heaven.

(Matthew 16:17–19)

And these signs will follow those who believe: In My name they will cast out demons; they will speak with new tongues; they will take up serpents; and if they drink anything deadly, it will by no means hurt them; they will lay hands on the sick, and they will recover.

(Mark 16:16)

I saw Satan fall like lightning from heaven. Behold, I give you the authority to trample on serpents and scorpions, and over all the power of the enemy, and nothing shall by any means hurt you. Nevertheless do not rejoice in this, that the spirits are subject to you, but rather rejoice because your names are written in heaven.

(Luke 10:18–20)

You did not choose Me, but I chose you and appointed you that you should go and bear fruit, and that your fruit should remain, that whatever you ask the Father in My name He may give you.

(John 15:16)

The Holy Spirit

Behold, I send the Promise of My Father upon you; but tarry in the city of Jerusalem until you are endued with power from on high.
(Luke 24:49)

And I will pray the Father, and He will give you another Helper, that He may abide with you forever—the Spirit of truth, whom the world cannot receive, because it neither sees Him nor knows Him; but you know Him, for He dwells with you and will be in you. I will not leave you orphans; I will come to you. A little while longer and the world will see Me no more, but you will see Me. Because I live, you will live also. At that day you will know that I am in My Father, and you in Me, and I in you.
(John 14:16–20)

And these things I have spoken to you while being present with you. But the Helper, the Holy Spirit, whom the Father will send in My name, He will teach you all things, and bring to your remembrance all things that I said to you.
(John 14:25–26)

But when the Helper comes, whom I shall send to you from the Father, the Spirit of truth who proceeds from the Father, He will testify of Me. And you also will bear witness, because you have been with Me from the beginning.

(John 15:26–27)

Nevertheless I tell you the truth. It is to your advantage that I go away; for if I do not go away, the Helper will not come to you; but if I depart, I will send Him to you. And when He has come, He will convict the world of sin, and of righteousness, and of judgment: of sin, because they do not believe in Me; of righteousness, because I go to My Father and you see Me no more; of judgment, because the ruler of this world is judged. I still have many things to say to you, but you cannot bear them now. However, when He, the Spirit of truth, has come, He will guide you into all truth; for He will not speak on His own authority, but whatever He hears He will speak; and He will tell you things to come. He will glorify Me, for He will take of what is Mine and declare it to you. All things that the Father has are Mine. Therefore I said that He will take of Mine and declare it to you.

(John 16:7–15)

For John truly baptized with water, but you shall be baptized with the Holy Spirit not many days from now.

(Acts 1:5)

But you shall receive power when the Holy Spirit has come upon you; and you shall be witnesses to Me in Jerusalem, and in all Judea and Samaria, and to the ends of the earth.

(Acts 1:8)

Peace and Rest

And do not fear those who kill the body but cannot kill the soul. But rather fear Him who is able to destroy both soul and body in hell. Are not two sparrows sold for a copper coin? And not one of them falls to the ground apart from your Father's will. But the very hairs of your head are all numbered. Do not fear therefore; you are of more value than many sparrows.

(Matthew 10:28–31; cf. Luke 12:3–7)

Come to Me, all you who labor and are heavy laden, and I will give you rest. Take My yoke upon you and learn from Me, for I am gentle and lowly in heart, and you will find rest for your souls. For My yoke is easy and My burden is light.

(Matthew 11:28–30)

Peace I leave with you, My peace I give to you; not as the world gives do I give to you. Let not your heart be troubled, neither let it be afraid.

(John 14:27)

A Place in Heaven

Let not your heart be troubled; you believe in God, believe also in Me. In My Father's house are many mansions; if it were not so, I would have told you. I go to prepare a place for you. And if I go and prepare a place for you, I will come again and receive you to Myself; that where I am, there you may be also. And where I go you know, and the way you know.

(John 14:1–4)

Rewards

🐋

Blessed are you when they revile and persecute you, and say all kinds of evil against you falsely for My sake. Rejoice and be exceedingly glad, for great is your reward in heaven, for so they persecuted the prophets who were before you.
(Matthew 5:11–12; cf. Luke 6:22, 23)

Take heed that you do not do your charitable deeds before men, to be seen by them. Otherwise you have no reward from your Father in heaven. But when you do a charitable deed, do not let your left hand know what your right hand is doing, that your charitable deed may be in secret; and your Father who sees in secret will Himself reward you openly.
(Matthew 6:1, 3–4)

Inheritance

છે.

And everyone who has left houses or brothers or sisters or father or mother or wife or children or lands, for My name's sake, shall receive a hundred-fold, and inherit eternal life.

(Matthew 19:29)

Then the King will say to those on His right hand, "Come, you blessed of My Father, inherit the king-dom prepared for you from the foundation of the world."

(Matthew 25:34)

———————————— ❧ ————————————

PRAYER

———————————— ❧ ————————————

Teaching on Prayer

❧

And when you pray, you shall not be like the hypocrites. For they love to pray standing in the synagogues and on the corners of the streets, that they may be seen by men. Assuredly, I say to you, they have their reward. But you, when you pray, go into your room, and when you have shut your door, pray to your Father who is in the secret place; and your Father who sees in secret will reward you openly. And when you pray, do not use vain repetitions as the heathen do. For they think that they will be heard for their many words. Therefore do not be like them. For your Father knows the things you have need of before you ask Him. In this manner, therefore, pray:

> Our Father in heaven,
> Hallowed be Your name.
> Your kingdom come.
> Your will be done
> On earth as it is in heaven.
> Give us this day our daily bread.
> And forgive us our debts,
> As we forgive our debtors.

And do not lead us into temptation,
But deliver us from the evil one.
For Yours is the kingdom and the
    power and the glory forever. Amen.

(Matthew 6:5–13; cf. Mark 11:25, Luke 11:2–4, 12:30)

What? Could you not watch with Me one hour?
Watch and pray, lest you enter into temptation. The
spirit indeed is willing, but the flesh is weak.

(Matthew 26:40–41; Mark 14:38, Luke 22:46)

His Own Prayers

I thank You, Father, Lord of heaven and earth, that You have hidden these things from the wise and prudent and have revealed them to babes. Even so, Father, for so it seemed good in Your sight.
(Matthew 11:25–26; cf. Luke 10:21)

O My Father, if it is possible, let this cup pass from Me; nevertheless, not as I will, but as You will. O My Father, if this cup cannot pass away from Me unless I drink it, Your will be done.
(Matthew 26:39, 42; Mark 14:36, Luke 22:42)

Father, I thank You that You have heard Me. And I know that You always hear Me, but because of the people who are standing by I said this, that they may believe that You sent Me.
(John 11:41–42)

Father, the hour has come. Glorify Your Son, that Your Son also may glorify You, as You have given Him authority over all flesh, that He should give eternal life to as many as You have given Him. And this is eternal life, that they may know You, the only true God, and Jesus Christ whom You have sent. I have glorified You on the earth. I have finished the work which You have given Me to do. And now, O Father, glorify Me together with Yourself, with the glory which I had with You before the world was. I have manifested Your name to the men whom You have given Me out of the world. They were Yours, You gave them to Me, and they have kept Your word. Now they have known that all things which You have given Me are from You. For I have given to them the words which You have given Me; and they have received them, and have known surely that I came forth from You; and they have believed that You sent Me. I pray for them. I do not pray for the world but for those whom You have given Me, for they are Yours. And all Mine are Yours, and Yours are Mine, and I am glorified in them. Now I am no longer in the world, but these are in the world, and I come to You. Holy Father, keep through Your name those whom You have given Me, that they may be one as We are. While I was with them in the world, I kept them in Your name. Those whom You gave Me I have kept; and none of them is lost except the son of perdition, that the Scripture might be fulfilled. But now I come to You, and these things I speak in the world, that they may have My joy fulfilled in themselves. I have given them Your word; and the world has hated them because they are not of the world, just as I am not of the world. I do not pray that You should take them out of the world, but that You should keep them from the evil one. They are not of the world, just as I am not of the world. Sanctify them by Your truth. Your word is truth. As You sent Me into the world, I also have sent them into the world. And for their sakes I sanctify Myself, that they also may be sanctified by the truth. I do not pray for these alone, but also for those who will believe in Me through their word; that they all may be one, as You, Father, are in Me, and I in You; that they also may be one in Us, that the world may believe that You sent Me. And the glory which You gave Me I have given them, that they may be one just as We are one: I in them, and You in Me; that they may be made perfect in one, and that the world may know that You have sent Me, and have loved them as You have loved Me. Father, I desire that they also whom You gave Me may be with Me where I am, that they may behold My glory which You have given Me; for You loved Me before the foundation of the world. O righteous Father! The world has not known You, but I have known You; and these have known that You sent Me. And I have declared to them Your name, and will declare it, that the love with which You loved Me may be in them, and I in them.

(John 17:1–26)

ADMONITIONS AND EXHORTATIONS

Calling His Disciples

❦

[*To Peter and Andrew*]

Follow Me, and I will make you fishers of men.
(Matthew 4:19; cf. Mark 1:17, Luke 5:10)

[*To others who would follow Him*]

Foxes have holes and birds of the air have nests, but
the Son of Man has nowhere to lay His head.
(Matthew 8:20; Luke 9:58)

Let the dead bury their own dead, but you go and
preach the kingdom of God.
(Luke 9:60; Matthew 8:22)

No one, having put his hand to the plow, and looking back, is fit for the kingdom of God.
(Luke 9:62)

Did I not choose you, the twelve, and one of you is
a devil?
(John 6:70)

Charge to His Disciples

๚

The harvest truly is plentiful, but the laborers are
few. Therefore pray the Lord of the harvest to send
out laborers into His harvest.
(Matthew 9:37–38; cf. Luke 10:2)

Do not go into the way of the Gentiles, and do not
enter a city of the Samaritans. But go rather to the
lost sheep of the house of Israel. And as you go,
preach, saying, "The kingdom of heaven is at
hand." Heal the sick, cleanse the lepers, raise the
dead, cast out demons. Freely you have received,
freely give. Provide neither gold nor silver nor copper in your moneybelts, nor bag for your journey,
nor two tunics, nor sandals, nor staffs; for a worker
is worthy of his food. Now whatever city or town
you enter, inquire who in it is worthy, and stay there
until you go out. And when you go into a household, greet it. If the household is worthy, let your
peace come upon it. But if it is not worthy, let your
peace return to you. And whoever will not receive
you nor hear your words, when you depart from
that house or city, shake off the dust from your feet.
Assuredly, I say to you, it will be more tolerable for

the land of Sodom and Gomorrah in the day of judgment than for that city!
(Matthew 10:5–15; cf. Mark 6:8–11, Luke 9:3–6)

Whatever I tell you in the dark, speak in the light; and what you hear in the ear, preach on the house-tops.
(Matthew 10:27; cf. Luke 12:3)

All authority has been given to Me in heaven and on earth. Go therefore and make disciples of all the nations, baptizing them in the name of the Father and of the Son and of the Holy Spirit, teaching them to observe all things that I have commanded you; and lo, I am with you always, even to the end of the age.
(Matthew 28:18–20)

Go into all the world and preach the gospel to every creature. He who believes and is baptized will be saved; but he who does not believe will be condemned. And these signs will follow those who believe: In My name they will cast out demons; they will speak with new tongues; they will take up serpents; and if they drink anything deadly, it will by no means hurt them; they will lay hands on the sick, and they will recover.
(Mark 16:15–16)

Do you not say, "There are still four months and then comes the harvest"? Behold, I say to you, lift up your eyes and look at the fields, for they are al-

ready white for harvest! And he who reaps receives
wages, and gathers fruit for eternal life, that both he
who sows and he who reaps may rejoice together.
For in this the saying is true: "One sows and another reaps." I sent you to reap that for which you
have not labored; others have labored, and you
have entered into their labors.

(John 4:35–38)

As the Father loved Me, I also have loved you; abide
in My love. If you keep My commandments, you
will abide in My love, just as I have kept My Father's
commandments and abide in His love. These things
I have spoken to you, that My joy may remain in
you, and that your joy may be full. This is My commandment, that you love one another as I have
loved you. Greater love has no one than this, than
to lay down one's life for his friends. You are My
friends if you do whatever I command you. No
longer do I call you servants, for a servant does not
know what his master is doing; but I have called
you friends, for all things that I heard from My
Father I have made known to you.

(John 15:9–15)

Peace to you! As the Father has sent Me, I also send
you. Receive the Holy Spirit. If you forgive the sins
of any, they are forgiven them; if you retain the sins
of any, they are retained.

(John 20:21–23)

Harsh Words
for the Religious System

❧

And I say to you that many will come from east and west, and sit down with Abraham, Isaac, and Jacob in the kingdom of heaven. But the sons of the kingdom will be cast out into outer darkness. There will be weeping and gnashing of teeth.

(Matthew 8:11–12; cf. Luke 13:28–29)

What did you go out into the wilderness to see? A reed shaken by the wind? But what did you go out to see? A man clothed in soft garments? Indeed, those who wear soft clothing are in kings' houses. But what did you go out to see? A prophet? Yes, I say to you, and more than a prophet. For this is he of whom it is written: "Behold, I send My messenger before Your face, who will prepare Your way before You." And from the days of John the Baptist until now the kingdom of heaven suffers violence, and the violent take it by force. For all the prophets and the law prophesied until John. And if you are willing to receive it, he is Elijah who is to come. He who has ears to hear, let him hear! But to what shall I liken this generation? It is like children sitting in the marketplaces and calling to their companions, and saying: "We played the flute for you, and you did not dance; we mourned to you, and you did not lament." For John came neither eating nor drinking, and they say, "He has a demon." The Son of Man came eating and drinking, and they say, "Look, a glutton and a winebibber, a friend of tax collectors and sinners!" But wisdom is justified by her children.

(Matthew 11:7–10, 12–19; cf. Luke 7:24–35)

Why do you also transgress the commandment of God because of your tradition? For God commanded, saying, "Honor your father and your mother"; and, "He who curses father or mother, let him be put to death." But you say, "Whoever says to his father or mother, 'Whatever profit you might have received from me is a gift to God'—then he need not honor his father or mother." Thus you have made the commandment of God of no effect by your tradition. Hypocrites! Well did Isaiah prophesy about you, saying: "These people draw near to me with their mouth, and honor Me with their lips, but their heart is far from Me. And in vain they worship Me, teaching as doctrines the commandments of men."

(Matthew 15:3–9; cf. Mark 7:6–13)

Every plant which My heavenly Father has not planted will be uprooted. Let them alone. They are blind leaders of the blind. And if the blind leads the blind, both will fall into a ditch.

(Matthew 15:13–14; cf. Luke 6:39)

O you of little faith, why do you reason among yourselves because you have brought no bread? Do you not yet understand, or remember the five loaves of the five thousand and how many baskets you took up? Nor the seven loaves of the four thousand and how many large baskets you took up? How is it you do not understand that I did not speak to you concerning bread?—but to beware of the leaven of the Pharisees and Sadducees.

(Matthew 16:8–11; cf. Mark 8:17–21)

Assuredly, I say to you that tax collectors and harlots enter the kingdom of God before you. For John came to you in the way of righteousness, and you did not believe him; but tax collectors and harlots believed him; and when you saw it, you did not afterward relent and believe him.

(Matthew 21:31–32)

Have you never read in the Scriptures: "The stone which the builders rejected has become the chief cornerstone. This was the Lord's doing, and it is marvelous in our eyes"? Therefore I say to you, the kingdom of God will be taken from you and given to a nation bearing the fruits of it. And whoever falls on this stone will be broken; but on whomever it falls, it will grind him to powder.

(Matthew 21:42–44)

The scribes and the Pharisees sit in Moses' seat. Therefore whatever they tell you to observe, that observe and do, but do not do according to their works; for they say, and do not do. For they bind heavy burdens, hard to bear, and lay them on men's shoulders; but they themselves will not move them with one of their fingers. But all their works they do to be seen by men. They make their phylacteries broad and enlarge the borders of their garments. They love the best places at feasts, the best seats in the synagogues, greetings in the marketplaces, and to be called by men, "Rabbi, Rabbi."

(Matthew 23:2–7; cf. Mark 12:38–39, Luke 11:43, 46)

But woe to you, scribes and Pharisees, hypocrites! For you shut up the kingdom of heaven against men; for you neither go in yourselves, nor do you allow those who are entering to go in. Woe to you, scribes and Pharisees, hypocrites! For you devour widows' houses, and for a pretense make long prayers. Therefore you will receive greater condemnation.

(Matthew 23:13–14; cf. Luke 11:52)

Woe to you, scribes and Pharisees, hypocrites! For you travel land and sea to win one proselyte, and when he is won, you make him twice as much a son of hell as yourselves.

(Matthew 23:15)

Woe to you, blind guides, who say, "Whoever swears by the temple, it is nothing; but whoever swears by the gold of the temple, he is obliged to perform it." Fools and blind! For which is greater, the gold or the temple that sanctifies the gold? And, "Whoever swears by the altar, it is nothing; but whoever swears by the gift that is on it, he is obliged to perform it." Fools and blind! For which is greater, the gift or the altar that sanctifies the gift? Therefore he who swears by the altar, swears by it and by all things on it. He who swears by the temple, swears by it and by Him who dwells in it. And he who swears by heaven, swears by the throne of God and by Him who sits on it.

(Matthew 23:16–22)

Woe to you, scribes and Pharisees, hypocrites! For you pay tithe of mint and anise and cummin, and have neglected the weightier matters of the law: justice and mercy and faith. These you ought to have done, without leaving the others undone. Blind guides, who strain out a gnat and swallow a camel!

(Matthew 23:23–24; cf. Luke 11:42)

Woe to you, scribes and Pharisees, hypocrites! For you cleanse the outside of the cup and dish, but inside they are full of extortion and self-indulgence. Blind Pharisee, first cleanse the inside of the cup and dish, that the outside of them may be clean also.

(Matthew 23:25–26; cf. Luke 11:39–41)

Woe to you, scribes and Pharisees, hypocrites! For you are like whitewashed tombs which indeed appear beautiful outwardly, but inside are full of dead men's bones and all uncleanness. Even so you also outwardly appear righteous to men, but inside you are full of hypocrisy and lawlessness.

(Matthew 23:27–28; cf. Luke 11:44)

Woe to you, scribes and Pharisees, hypocrites! Because you build the tombs of the prophets and adorn the monuments of the righteous, and say, "If we had lived in the days of our fathers, we would not have been partakers with them in the blood of the prophets." Therefore you are witnesses against yourselves that you are sons of those who murdered the prophets. Fill up, then, the measure of your fathers' guilt. Serpents, brood of vipers! How can you escape the condemnation of hell? Therefore, indeed, I send you prophets, wise men, and scribes: some of them you will kill and crucify, and some of them you will scourge in your synagogues and persecute from city to city, that on you may come all the righteous blood shed on the earth, from the blood of righteous Abel to the blood of

Zechariah, son of Berechiah, whom you murdered between the temple and the altar. Assuredly, I say to you, all these things will come upon this generation.

(Matthew 23:29–36; cf. Luke 11:47–51)

Woe to you also, lawyers! For you load men with burdens hard to bear, and you yourselves do not touch the burdens with one of your fingers.

(Luke 11:46)

Woe to you lawyers! For you have taken away the key of knowledge. You did not enter in yourselves, and those who were entering in you hindered.

(Luke 11:52)

Beware of the leaven of the Pharisees, which is hypocrisy. For there is nothing covered that will not be revealed, nor hidden that will not be known. Therefore whatever you have spoken in the dark will be heard in the light, and what you have spoken in the ear in inner rooms will be proclaimed on the housetops.

(Luke 12:1–3, cf. Matthew 10:26–27, 16:6, Mark 4:22, 8:15)

[In response to objections for healing on the sabbath]

Hypocrite! Does not each one of you on the Sabbath loose his ox or donkey from the stall, and lead it away to water it? So ought not this woman, being a daughter of Abraham, whom Satan has bound—

think of it—for eighteen years, be loosed from this bond on the Sabbath?

(Luke 13:15–16)

You are those who justify yourselves before men, but God knows your hearts. For what is highly esteemed among men is an abomination in the sight of God. The law and the prophets were until John. Since that time the kingdom of God has been preached, and everyone is pressing into it. And it is easier for heaven and earth to pass away than for one tittle of the law to fail.

(Luke 16:15–17; cf. Matthew 5:18, 11:12–13)

It is written, "My house is a house of prayer," but you have made it a "den of thieves."

(Luke 19:46; cf. Matthew 21:13, Mark 11:17, John 2:16)

[*To Nicodemus*]

Are you the teacher of Israel, and do not know these things? Most assuredly, I say to you, We speak what We know and testify what We have seen, and you do not receive Our witness. If I have told you earthly things and you do not believe, how will you believe if I tell you heavenly things? No one has ascended to heaven but He who came down from heaven, that is, the Son of Man who is in heaven.

(John 3:10–13)

I do not receive honor from men. But I know you, that you do not have the love of God in you. I have come in My Father's name, and you do not receive Me; if another comes in his own name, him you will receive. How can you believe, who receive honor from one another, and do not seek the honor that comes from the only God? Do not think that I shall accuse you to the Father; there is one who accuses you—Moses, in whom you trust. For if you believed Moses, you would believe Me; for he wrote about Me. But if you do not believe his writings, how will you believe My words?

(John 5:41–47)

You are from beneath, I am from above. You are of this world; I am not of this world. Therefore I said to you that you will die in your sins; for if you do not believe that I am He, you will die in your sins.

(John 8:23–24)

I know that you are Abraham's descendants, but you seek to kill Me, because My word has no place in you. I speak what I have seen with My Father, and you do what you have seen with your father. If you were Abraham's children, you would do the works of Abraham. But now you seek to kill Me, a Man who has told you the truth which I heard from God. Abraham did not do this. You do the deeds of your father.

(John 8:37–41)

Why do you not understand my speech? Because you are not able to listen to My word. You are of your father the devil, and the desires of your father you want to do. He was a murderer from the beginning, and does not stand in the truth, because there is no truth in him. When he speaks a lie, he speaks from his own resources, for he is a liar and the father of it. But because I tell the truth, you do not believe Me. Which of you convicts Me of sin? And if I tell the truth, why do you not believe Me? He who is of God hears God's words; therefore you do not hear, because you are not of God.

(John 8:43–47)

If you were blind, you would have no sin; but now you say, "We see." Therefore your sin remains.

(John 9:41)

Laments for the Cities of Israel

❧

Woe to you, Chorazin! Woe to you, Bethsaida! For if the mighty works which were done in you had been done in Tyre and Sidon, they would have repented long ago in sackcloth and ashes. But I say to you, it will be more tolerable for Tyre and Sidon in the day of judgment than for you.

(Matthew 11:21–22; cf. Luke 10:13–14)

And you, Capernaum, who are exalted to heaven, will be brought down to Hades; for if the mighty works which were done in you had been done in Sodom, it would have remained until this day. But I say to you that it shall be more tolerable for the land of Sodom in the day of judgment than for you.

(Matthew 11:23–24; cf. Luke 10:12, 15)

O Jerusalem, Jerusalem, the one who kills the prophets and stones those who are sent to her! How often I wanted to gather your children together, as a hen gathers her chicks under her wings, but you were not willing! See! Your house is left to you desolate; for I say to you, you shall see Me no more till you say, "Blessed is He who comes in the name of the Lord!"

(Matthew 23:37–39; cf. Luke 13:34–35)

[*Regarding Jerusalem*]

If you had known, even you, especially in this your day, the things that make for your peace! But now they are hidden from your eyes. For days will come upon you when your enemies will build an embankment around you, surround you and close you in on every side, and level you, and your children within you, to the ground; and they will not leave in you one stone upon another, because you did not know the time of your visitation.

(Luke 19:42–44)

Judgment

ã♥

[Regarding an atrocity involving Galileans]

Do you suppose that these Galileans were worse sinners than all other Galileans, because they suffered such things? I tell you, no; but unless you repent you will all likewise perish. Or those eighteen on whom the tower in Siloam fell and killed them, do you think that they were worse sinners than all other men who dwelt in Jerusalem? I tell you, no; but unless you repent you will all likewise perish.
(Luke 13:2–5)

Words on the Cross

&

Eli, Eli, lama sabachthani? My God, My God, why have You forsaken Me?
(Matthew 27:46; cf. Mark 15:34)

Father, forgive them, for they do not know what they do.
(Luke 23:34)

[*To the thief beside Him*]
Assuredly, I say to you, today you will be with Me in Paradise.
(Luke 23:43)

Father, into Your hands I commit My spirit.
(Luke 23:46)

[*To His mother*]
Woman, behold your son!
(John 19:26)

[*To His disciple John*]
Behold your mother!
(John 19:27)

I thirst!

(John 19:28)

It is finished!

(John 19:30)

PREDICTIONS

His Rejection and Death

❧

Indeed, Elijah is coming first and will restore all things. But I say to you that Elijah has come already, and they did not know him but did to him whatever they wished. Likewise the Son of Man is also about to suffer at their hands.

(Matthew 17:11–12; cf. Mark 9:12–13)

The Son of Man is about to be betrayed into the hands of men, and they will kill Him, and the third day He will be raised up.

(Matthew 17:22–23; cf. Mark 9:31, Luke 9:44, John 2:19)

Behold, we are going up to Jerusalem, and the Son of Man will be betrayed to the chief priests and to the scribes; and they will condemn Him to death, and deliver Him to the Gentiles to mock and to scourge and to crucify. And the third day He will rise again.

(Matthew 20:18–19; cf. Mark 10:33–34, Luke 18:31–33)

You know that after two days is the Passover, and the Son of Man will be delivered up to be crucified.

(Matthew 26:2)

Why do you trouble the woman? For she has done a good work for Me. For you have the poor with you always, but Me you do not have always. For in pouring this fragrant oil on My body, she did it for My burial. Assuredly, I say to you, wherever this gospel is preached in the whole world, what this woman has done will also be told as a memorial to her.
(Matthew 26:10–13; cf. Mark 14:3, John 12:1–8)

Assuredly, I say to you, one of you will betray Me. He who dipped his hand with Me in the dish will betray Me. The Son of Man indeed goes just as it is written of Him, but woe to that man by whom the Son of Man is betrayed! It would have been good for that man if he had not been born.
(Matthew 26:21–24; cf. Mark 14:18–21, Luke 22:21–22)

All of you will be made to stumble because of Me this night, for it is written: "I will strike the Shepherd, and the sheep of the flock will be scattered."
(Matthew 26:31; cf. Mark 14:27)

Are you still sleeping and resting? Behold, the hour is at hand, and the Son of Man is being betrayed into the hands of sinners. Rise, let us be going. See, My betrayer is at hand.
(Matthew 26:45–46; cf. Mark 14:41–42)

You will surely say this proverb to Me, "Physician, heal yourself! Whatever we have heard done in Capernaum, do also here in Your country." Assuredly, I say to you, no prophet is accepted in his own country. But I tell you truly, many widows were in Israel in the days of Elijah, when the heaven was shut up three years and six months, and there was a great famine throughout all the land; but to none of them was Elijah sent except to Zarephath, in the region of Sidon, to a woman who was a widow. And many lepers were in Israel in the time of Elisha the prophet, and none of them was cleansed except Naaman the Syrian.

(Luke 4:23–27; cf. Matthew 13:57, Mark 6:4)

The Son of Man must suffer many things, and be rejected by the elders and chief priests and scribes, and be killed, and be raised the third day.

(Luke 9:22)

[Upon being told of Herod's desire to kill Him]

Go, tell that fox, "Behold, I cast out demons and perform cures today and tomorrow, and the third day I shall be perfected." Nevertheless I must journey today, tomorrow, and the day following; for it cannot be that a prophet should perish outside of Jerusalem.

(Luke 13:32–33)

And as Moses lifted up the serpent in the wilderness, even so must the Son of Man be lifted up, that

whoever believes in Him should not perish but
have eternal life.

(John 3:14–15)

[*In defense of the woman who anointed His feet*]

Let her alone; she has kept this for the day of My
burial. For the poor you have with you always, but
Me you do not have always.

(John 12:7–8)

Now is the judgment of this world; now the ruler of
this world will be cast out. And I, if I am lifted up
from the earth, will draw all peoples to Myself.

(John 12:31–32)

I do not speak concerning all of you. I know whom
I have chosen; but that the Scripture may be fulfilled, "He who eats bread with Me has lifted up his
heel against Me." Now I tell you before it comes,
that when it does come to pass, you may believe
that I am He.

(John 13:18–19)

Most assuredly, I say to you, one of you will betray
Me.

(John 13:21)

Where I am going you cannot follow Me now, but
you shall follow Me afterward.

(John 13:36)

I will no longer talk much with you, for the ruler of this world is coming, and he has nothing in Me. But that the world may know that I love the Father, and as the Father gave Me commandment, so I do.

(John 14:30–31)

A little while, and you will not see Me; and again a little while, and you will see Me, because I go to the Father.

(John 16:16)

Put your sword into the sheath. Shall I not drink the cup which My Father has given Me?

(John 18:11)

His Resurrection

꙳

Tell the vision to no one until the Son of Man is
risen from the dead.
(Matthew 17:9)

But after I have been raised, I will go before you to
Galilee.
(Matthew 26:32; cf. Mark 14:28)

Destroy this temple, and in three days I will raise it
up.
(John 2:19)

His Ascension and Glorification

૨ક

Can the friends of the bridegroom mourn as long as the bridegroom is with them? But the days will come when the bridegroom will be taken away from them, and then they will fast.

(Matthew 9:15; cf. Mark 2:19–20, Luke 5:34–35)

I shall be with you a little while longer, and then I go to Him who sent Me. You will seek Me and not find Me, and where I am you cannot come.

(John 7:33–34)

I am going away, and you will seek Me, and will die in your sin. Where I go you cannot come.

(John 8:21)

Now the Son of Man is glorified, and God is glorified in Him. If God is glorified in Him, God will also glorify Him in Himself, and glorify Him immediately. Little children, I shall be with you a little while longer. You will seek Me; and as I said to the Jews,

"Where I am going, you cannot come," so now I say to you.
(John 13:31–33)

You have heard Me say to you, "I am going away and coming back to you." If you loved Me, you would rejoice because I said, "I am going to the Father," for My Father is greater than I. And now I have told you before it comes, that when it does come to pass, you may believe.
(John 14:28–29)

But now I go away to Him who sent Me, and none of you asks Me, "Where are You going?" But because I have said these things to you, sorrow has filled your heart.
(John 16:5–6)

Are you inquiring among yourselves about what I said, "A little while, and you will not see Me; and again a little while, and you will see Me"? Most assuredly, I say to you that you will weep and lament, but the world will rejoice; and you will be sorrowful, but your sorrow will be turned into joy. A woman, when she is in labor, has sorrow because her hour has come; but as soon as she has given birth to the child, she no longer remembers the anguish, for joy that a human being has been born into the world. Therefore you now have sorrow; but I will see you again and your heart will rejoice, and your joy no one will take from you. And in that day you will ask Me nothing. Most assuredly, I say to you, whatever you ask the Father in My name He will give you. Until now you have asked nothing in My name. Ask, and you will receive, that your joy may be full. These things I have spoken to you in figurative language; but the time is coming when I will no longer speak to you in figurative language, but I will tell you plainly about the Father. In that day you will ask in My name, and I do not say to you that I shall pray the Father for you; for the Father Himself loves you, because you have loved Me, and have believed that I came forth from God. I came forth from the Father and have come into the world. Again, I leave the world and go to the Father. (John 16:19–28)

Do not cling to Me, for I have not yet ascended to My Father; but go to My brethren and say to them, "I am ascending to My Father and your Father, and to My God and your God."
(John 20:17)

Persecution of
His Followers

❧

Behold, I send you out as sheep in the midst of wolves. Therefore be wise as serpents and harmless as doves. But beware of men, for they will deliver you up to councils and scourge you in their synagogues. You will be brought before governors and kings for My sake, as a testimony to them and to the Gentiles. But when they deliver you up, do not worry about how or what you should speak. For it will be given to you in that hour what you should speak; for it is not you who speak, but the Spirit of your Father who speaks in you. Now brother will deliver up brother to death, and a father his child; and children will rise up against parents and cause them to be put to death. And you will be hated by all for My name's sake. But he who endures to the end will be saved. When they persecute you in this city, flee to another. For assuredly, I say to you, you will not have gone through the cities of Israel before the Son of Man comes.

(Matthew 10:16–23; cf. Mark 13:9–13, Luke 10:3, 21:11–19)

A disciple is not above his teacher, nor a servant above his master. It is enough for a disciple that he be like his teacher, and a servant like his master. If they have called the master of the house Beelzebub, how much more will they call those of his household! Therefore do not fear them. For there is nothing covered that will not be revealed, and hidden that will not be known.

(Matthew 10:24–26; cf. Mark 4:22, Luke 6:40, 8:17, 12:2)

If the world hates you, you know that it hated Me before it hated you. If you were of the world, the world would love its own. Yet because you are not of the world, but I chose you out of the world, therefore the world hates you. Remember the word that I said to you, "A servant is not greater than his master." If they persecuted Me, they will also persecute you. If they kept My word, they will keep yours also. But all these things they will do to you for My name's sake, because they do not know Him who sent Me.

(John 15:18–21)

These things I have spoken to you, that you should not be made to stumble. They will put you out of the synagogues; yes, the time is coming that whoever kills you will think that he offers God service. And these things they will do to you because they have not known the Father nor Me. But these things I have told you, that when the time comes, you may remember that I told you of them. And these things I did not say to you at the beginning, because I was with you.

(John 16:1–4)

Indeed the hour is coming, yes, has now come, that you will be scattered, each to his own, and will leave Me alone. And yet I am not alone, because the Father is with Me. These things I have spoken to you, that in Me you may have peace. In the world you will have tribulation; but be of good cheer, I have overcome the world.

(John 16:32–33)

The Resurrection of the Saints

❧

The sons of this age marry and are given in marriage. But those who are accounted worthy to attain that age, and the resurrection from the dead, neither marry nor are given in marriage; nor can they die anymore, for they are equal to the angels and are sons of God, being sons of the resurrection. But even Moses showed in the burning bush passage that the dead are raised, when he called the Lord "the God of Abraham, the God of Isaac, and the God of Jacob." For He is not the God of the dead but of the living, for all live to Him.

(Luke 20:34–38; cf. Matthew 22:29–32, Mark 12:24–27)

Most assuredly, I say to you, the hour is coming, and now is, when the dead will hear the voice of the Son of God; and those who hear will live. For as the Father has life in Himself, so He has granted the Son to have life in Himself, and has given Him authority to execute judgment also, because He is the Son of Man. Do not marvel at this; for the hour is coming in which all who are in the graves will hear His voice and shall come forth—those who have done good, to the resurrection of life, and those who have done evil, to the resurrection of condemnation.

(John 5:25–29)

His Coming in Glory

ટે⋅

For the Son of Man will come in the glory of His
Father with His angels, and then He will reward
each according to his works. Assuredly, I say to you,
there are some standing here who shall not taste
death till they see the Son of Man coming in His
kingdom.

(Matthew 16:27–28; cf. Mark 9:1, Luke 9:27)

With fervent desire I have desired to eat this Passover with you before I suffer; for I say to you, I will
no longer eat of it until it is fulfilled in the kingdom
of God. Take this [*cup*] and divide it among yourselves; for I say to you, I will not drink of the fruit of
the vine until the kingdom of God comes.

(Luke 22:15–18; cf. Matthew 26:29, Mark 14:25)

Most assuredly, I say to you, hereafter you shall see
heaven open, and the angels of God ascending and
descending upon the Son of Man.

(John 1:51)

Let not your heart be troubled; you believe in God,
believe also in Me. In My Father's house are many

mansions; if it were not so, I would have told you. I go to prepare a place for you. And if I go and prepare a place for you, I will come again and receive you to Myself; that where I am, there you may be also. And where I go you know, and the way you know.

(John 14:1–4)

The End of the Age

٨

Do you not see all these things? Assuredly, I say to you, not one stone shall be left here upon another, that shall not be thrown down. Take heed that no one deceives you. For many will come in My name, saying, "I am the Christ," and will deceive many. And you will hear of wars and rumors of wars. See that you are not troubled; for all these things must come to pass, but the end is not yet. For nation will rise against nation, and kingdom against kingdom. And there will be famines, pestilences, and earthquakes in various places. All these are the beginning of sorrows. Then they will deliver you up to tribulation and kill you, and you will be hated by all nations for My name's sake. And then many will be offended, will betray one another, and will hate one another. Then many false prophets will rise up and deceive many. And because lawlessness will abound, the love of many will grow cold. But he who endures to the end shall be saved. And this gospel of the kingdom will be preached in all the world as a witness to all the nations, and then the end will come.

(Matthew 24:2–14; cf. Mark 13:2–13, Luke 21:6–19)

Therefore when you see the "abomination of desolation," spoken of by Daniel the prophet, standing in the holy place (whoever reads, let him understand), then let those who are in Judea flee to the mountains. Let him who is on the housetop not go down to get anything out of his house. And let him who is in the field not go back to get his clothes. But woe to those who are pregnant and to those who are nursing babies in those days! And pray that your flight may not be in winter or on the Sabbath. For then there will be great tribulation, such as has not been since the beginning of the world until this time, no, nor ever shall be. And unless those days were shortened, no flesh would be saved; but for the elect's sake those days will be shortened. Then if anyone says to you, "Look, here is the Christ!" or "There!" do not believe it.

(Matthew 24:15–23; cf. Mark 13:14–21, Luke 21:20–24)

For false christs and false prophets will rise and show great signs and wonders to deceive, if possible, even the elect. See, I have told you beforehand. Therefore if they say to you, "Look, He is in the desert!" do not go out; or "Look, He is in the inner rooms!" do not believe it. For as the lightning comes from the east and flashes to the west, so also will the coming of the Son of Man be. For wherever the carcass is, there the eagles will be gathered together.

(Matthew 24:24–28; cf. Mark 13:22–23, Luke 17:23–24, 37)

Immediately after the tribulation of those days the sun will be darkened, and the moon will not give its light; the stars will fall from heaven, and the powers of the heavens will be shaken. Then the sign of the Son of Man will appear in heaven, and then all the tribes of the earth will mourn, and they will see the Son of Man coming on the clouds of heaven with power and great glory. And He will send His angels with a great sound of a trumpet and they will gather together His elect from the four winds, from one end of heaven to the other.

(Matthew 24:29–31; cf. Mark 13:24–27, Luke 21:25–28)

Now learn this parable from the fig tree: When its branch has already become tender and puts forth leaves, you know that summer is near. So you also, when you see all these things, know that it is near—at the doors! Assuredly, I say to you, this generation will by no means pass away till all these things take place. Heaven and earth will pass away, but My words will by no means pass away. But of that day and hour no one knows, not even the angels of heaven, but My Father only. But as the days of Noah were, so also will the coming of the Son of Man be. For as in the days before the flood, they were eating and drinking, marrying and giving in marriage, until the day that Noah entered the ark, and did not know until the flood came and took them all away, so also will the coming of the Son of Man be. Then two men will be in the field: one will be taken and the other left. Two women will be grinding at the mill: one will be taken and the other left.

(Matthew 24:32–41; cf. Mark 13:28–32, Luke 17:26–27, 21:29–33, 34–35)

Let your waist be girded and your lamps burning; and you yourselves be like men who wait for their master, when he will return from the wedding, that when he comes and knocks they may open to him immediately. Blessed are those servants whom the master, when he comes, will find watching. Assuredly, I say to you that he will gird himself and have them sit down to eat, and will come and serve them. And if he should come in the second watch, or come in the third watch, and find them so, blessed are those servants. But know this, that if the master of the house had known what hour the thief would come, he would have watched and not allowed his house to be broken into. Therefore you also be ready, for the Son of Man is coming at an hour you do not expect.

(Luke 12:35–40; cf. Matthew 24:42–44)

Who then is that faithful and wise steward, whom his master will make ruler over his household, to give them their portion of food in due season? Blessed is that servant whom his master will find so doing when he comes. Truly, I say to you that he will make him ruler over all that he has. But if that servant says in his heart, "My master is delaying his coming," and begins to beat the male and female servants, and to eat and drink and be drunk, the master of that servant will come on a day when he is not looking for him, and at an hour when he is not aware, and will cut him in two and appoint him his portion with the unbelievers. And that servant who knew his master's will, and did not prepare himself or do according to his will, shall be beaten with many stripes. But he who did not know, yet committed things deserving of stripes, shall be beaten with few. For everyone to whom much is given, from him much will be required; and to whom much has been committed, of him they will ask the more.

(Luke 12:42–48; cf. Matthew 24:45–51)

And Jerusalem will be trampled by Gentiles until the times of the Gentiles are fulfilled.

(Luke 21:24)

But take heed to yourselves, lest your hearts be weighed down with carousing, drunkenness, and cares of this life, and that Day come on you unexpectedly. For it will come as a snare on all those who dwell on the face of the whole earth. Watch therefore, and pray always that you may be counted worthy to escape all these things that will come to pass, and to stand before the Son of Man.

(Luke 21:34–36)

It is not for you to know times or seasons which the Father has put in His own authority.

(Acts 1:7)

Various Other Predictions

꿈

Go into the village opposite you, and immediately you will find a donkey tied, and a colt with her. Loose them and bring them to Me. And if anyone says anything to you, you shall say, "The Lord has need of them," and immediately he will send them.
(Matthew 21:2–3; cf. Mark 11:2–3, Luke 19:29–30)

Behold, when you have entered the city, a man will meet you carrying a pitcher of water; follow him into the house which he enters. Then you shall say to the master of the house, "The Teacher says to you, 'Where is the guest room where I may eat the Passover with My disciples?'" Then he will show you a large, furnished upper room; there make ready.
(Luke 22:10–12; cf. Matthew 26:18, Mark 14:13–15)

Simon, Simon! Indeed, Satan has asked for you, that he may sift you as wheat. But I have prayed for you, that your faith should not fail; and when you have returned to Me, strengthen your brethren. I

tell you, Peter, the rooster shall not crow this day before you will deny three times that you know Me.
(Luke 22:31–32, 34; cf. Matthew 26:34, Mark 14:30)

Daughters of Jerusalem, do not weep for Me, but weep for yourselves and for your children. For indeed the days are coming in which they will say, "Blessed are the barren, wombs that never bore, and breasts which never nursed!" Then they will begin to say to the mountains, "Fall on us!" and to the hills, "Cover us!" For if they do these things in the green wood, what will be done in the dry?
(Luke 23:28–31)

[*To Peter*]

Will you lay down your life for My sake? Most assuredly, I say to you, the rooster shall not crow till you have denied Me three times.
(John 13:38)

[*To Peter*]

Most assuredly, I say to you, when you were younger, you girded yourself and walked where you wished; but when you are old, you will stretch out your hands, and another will gird you and carry you where you do not wish.
(John 21:18)

---- ❧ ----

PARABLES

---- ❧ ----

The Radical Nature of His Message

❧

The New and the Old Wineskins

No one puts a piece from a new garment on an old one; otherwise the new makes a tear, and also the piece that was taken out of the new does not match the old. And no one puts new wine into old wineskins; or else the new wine will burst the wineskins and be spilled, and the wineskins will be ruined. But new wine must be put into new wineskins, and both are preserved. And no one, having drunk old wine, immediately desires new; for he says, "The old is better."

(Luke 5:36–39; cf. Matthew 9:16–17, Mark 2:21–22)

The Response to His Message

❧

The Sower

Behold, a sower went out to sow. And as he sowed, some seed fell by the wayside; and the birds came and devoured them. Some fell on stony places, where they did not have much earth; and they immediately sprang up because they had no depth of earth. But when the sun was up they were scorched, and because they had no root they withered away. And some fell among thorns, and the thorns sprang up and choked them. But others fell on good ground and yielded a crop: some a hundredfold, some sixty, some thirty. He who has ears to hear, let him hear.

(Matthew 13:3–9; cf. Mark 4:3–9, Luke 8:5–8)

Therefore hear the parable of the sower: When anyone hears the word of the kingdom, and does not understand it, then the wicked one comes and snatches away what was sown in his heart. This is he who received seed by the wayside. But he who received the seed on stony places, this is he who hears the word and immediately receives it with joy; yet he has no root in himself, but endures only for a while. For when tribulation or persecution arises because of the word, immediately he stumbles. Now he who received seed among the thorns is he who hears the word, and the cares of this world and the deceitfulness of riches choke the word, and he becomes unfruitful. But he who received seed on the good ground is he who hears the word and understands it, who indeed bears fruit and produces: some a hundredfold, some sixty, some thirty.

(Matthew 13:18–23; cf. Mark 4:13–20, Luke 8:11–15)

His Rejection

❧

The Wicked Tenants

There was a certain landowner who planted a vineyard and set a hedge around it, dug a winepress in it and built a tower. And he leased it to vinedressers and went into a far country. Now when vintage-time drew near, he sent his servants to the vinedressers, that they might receive its fruit. And the vinedressers took his servants, beat one, killed one, and stoned another. Again he sent other servants, more than the first, and they did likewise to them. Then last of all he sent his son to them, saying, "They will respect my son." But when the vinedressers saw the son, they said among themselves, "This is the heir. Come, let us kill him and seize his inheritance." So they took him and cast him out of the vineyard and killed him. Therefore, when the owner of the vineyard comes, what will he do to those vinedressers?

(Matthew 21:33–40; cf. Mark 12:1–11, Luke 20:9–18)

Being Prepared for the End

Wise and Foolish Builders

Therefore whoever hears these sayings of Mine, and does them, I will liken him to a wise man who built his house on the rock: and the rain descended, the floods came, and the winds blew and beat on that house; and it did not fall, for it was founded on the rock. But everyone who hears these sayings of Mine, and does not do them, will be like a foolish man who built his house on the sand: and the rain descended, the floods came, and the winds blew and beat on that house; and it fell. And great was its fall.

(Matthew 7:24–27; cf. Luke 6:47–49)

Marriage Guest Ejected

The kingdom of heaven is like a certain king who arranged a marriage for his son, and sent out his servants to call those who were invited to the wedding; and they were not willing to come. Again, he sent out other servants, saying, "Tell those who are invited, 'See, I have prepared my dinner; my oxen and fatted cattle are killed, and all things are ready. Come to the wedding.'" But they made light of it and went their ways, one to his own farm, another to his business. And the rest seized his servants, treated them spitefully, and killed them. But when the king heard about it, he was furious. And he sent out his armies, destroyed those murderers, and burned up their city. Then he said to his servants, "The wedding is ready, but those who were invited were not worthy. Therefore go into the highways, and as many as you find, invite to the wedding." So those servants went out into the highways and gathered together all whom they found, both bad and good. And the wedding hall was filled with guests. But when the king came in to see the guests, he saw a man there who did not have on a wedding garment. So he said to him, "Friend, how did you come in here without a wedding garment?" And he was speechless. Then the king said to the servants, "Bind him hand and foot, take him away, and cast him into outer darkness; there will be weeping and gnashing of teeth." For many are called, but few are chosen.

(Matthew 22:2–14)

The Ten Virgins

Then the kingdom of heaven shall be likened to ten virgins who took their lamps and went out to meet the bridegroom. Now five of them were wise, and five were foolish. Those who were foolish took their lamps and took no oil with them, but the wise took oil in their vessels with their lamps. But while the bridegroom was delayed, they all slumbered and slept. And at midnight a cry was heard: "Behold, the bridegroom is coming; go out to meet him!" Then all those virgins arose and trimmed their lamps. And the foolish said to the wise, "Give us some of your oil, for our lamps are going out." But the wise answered, saying, "No, lest there should not be enough for us and for you; but go rather to those who sell, and buy for yourselves." And while they went to buy, the bridegroom came, and those who were ready went in with him to the wedding; and the door was shut. Afterward the other virgins came also, saying, "Lord, Lord, open to us!" But he answered and said, "Assuredly, I say to you, I do not know you." Watch therefore, for you know neither the day nor the hour in which the Son of Man is coming.

(Matthew 25:1–13)

The Foolish Rich Man

The ground of a certain rich man yielded plentifully. And he thought within himself, saying, "What shall I do, since I have no room to store my crops?" So he said, "I will do this: I will pull down my barns and build greater, and there I will store all my crops and my goods. And I will say to my soul, 'Soul, you have many goods laid up for many years; take your ease; eat, drink, and be merry.'" But God said to him, "Fool! This night your soul will be required of you; then whose will those things be which you have provided?" So is he who lays up treasure for himself, and is not rich toward God.

(Luke 12:16–21)

Stewardship and Bearing Fruit

۶۹

Good and Bad Stewards

For the kingdom of heaven is like a man traveling to a far country, who called his own servants and delivered his goods to them. And to one he gave five talents, to another two, and to another one, to each according to his own ability; and immediately he went on a journey. Then he who had received the five talents went and traded with them, and made another five talents. And likewise he who had received two gained two more also. But he who had received one went and dug in the ground, and hid his lord's money. After a long time the lord of those servants came and settled accounts with them. So he who had received five talents came and brought five other talents, saying, "Lord, you delivered to me five talents; look, I have gained five more talents besides them." His lord said to him, "Well done, good and faithful servant; you were faithful over a few things, I will make you ruler over many things. Enter into the joy of your lord." He also who had received two talents came and said, "Lord, you de-

livered to me two talents; look, I have gained two
more talents besides them." His lord said to him,
"Well done, good and faithful servant; you have
been faithful over a few things, I will make you ruler
over many things. Enter into the joy of your lord."
Then he who had received the one talent came and
said, "Lord, I knew you to be a hard man, reaping
where you have not sown, and gathering where
you have not scattered seed. And I was afraid, and
went and hid your talent in the ground. Look, there
you have what is yours." But his lord answered and
said to him, "You wicked and lazy servant, you
knew that I reap where I have not sown, and gather
where I have not scattered seed. So you ought to
have deposited my money with the bankers, and at
my coming I would have received back my own
with interest. Therefore take the talent from him,
and give it to him who has ten talents. For to everyone who has, more will be given, and he will have
abundance; but from him who does not have, even
what he has will be taken away. And cast the unprofitable servant into the outer darkness. There will be
weeping and gnashing of teeth."

(Matthew 25:14–30; cf. Luke 19:12–27)

The Fig Tree

A certain man had a fig tree planted in his vineyard,
and he came seeking fruit on it and found none.
Then he said to the keeper of his vineyard, "Look,
for three years I have come seeking fruit on this fig

tree and find none. Cut it down; why does it use up the ground?" But he answered and said to him, "Sir, let it alone this year also, until I dig around it and fertilize it. And if it bears fruit, well. But if not, after that you can cut it down."

(Luke 13:6–9)

The Clever but Evil Steward

There was a certain rich man who had a steward, and an accusation was brought to him that this man was wasting his goods. So he called him and said to him, "What is this I hear about you? Give an account of your stewardship, for you can no longer be steward." Then the steward said within himself, "What shall I do? For my master is taking the stewardship away from me. I cannot dig; I am ashamed to beg. I have resolved what to do, that when I am put out of the stewardship, they may receive me into their houses." So he called every one of his master's debtors to him, and said to the first, "How much do you owe my master?" And he said, "A hundred measures of oil." So he said to him, "Take your bill, and sit down quickly and write fifty." Then he said to another, "And how much do you owe?" So he said, "A hundred measures of wheat." And he said to him, "Take your bill, and write eighty." So the master commended the unjust steward because he had dealt shrewdly. For the sons of this world are more shrewd in their generation than the sons of light. And I say to you, make friends for yourselves by unrighteous mammon, that when you fail, they may receive you into an everlasting home. He who is faithful in what is least is faithful also in much; and he who is unjust in what is least is unjust also in much. Therefore if you have not been faithful in the unrighteous mammon, who will commit to your trust the true riches? And if you have not been faithful in what is another man's, who will give you what is your own? No servant can serve two masters; for either he will hate the one and love the other, or else he will be loyal to the one and despise the other. You cannot serve God and mammon.

(Luke 16:1–13)

Obedience

෴

The Two Sons

But what do you think? A man had two sons, and he came to the first and said, "Son, go, work today in my vineyard." He answered and said, "I will not," but afterward he regretted it and went. Then he came to the second and said likewise. And he answered and said, "I go, sir," but he did not go. Which of the two did the will of his father?

(Matthew 21:28–31)

True Religion

&❧

The Good Samaritan

A certain man went down from Jerusalem to
Jericho, and fell among thieves, who stripped him
of his clothing, wounded him, and departed, leaving him half dead. Now by chance a certain priest
came down that road. And when he saw him, he
passed by on the other side. Likewise a Levite,
when he arrived at the place, came and looked, and
passed by on the other side. But a certain Samaritan, as he journeyed, came where he was. And
when he saw him, he had compassion. So he went
to him and bandaged his wounds, pouring on oil
and wine; and he set him on his own animal,
brought him to an inn, and took care of him. On the
next day, when he departed, he took out two denarii [*two days' wages*], gave them to the innkeeper,
and said to him, "Take care of him; and whatever
more you spend, when I come again, I will repay
you." So which of these three do you think was
neighbor to him who fell among the thieves? Go
and do likewise.

(Luke 10:30–37)

The Pharisee and the Tax-Collector

Two men went up to the temple to pray, one a Pharisee and the other a tax-collector. The Pharisee stood and prayed thus with himself, "God, I thank You that I am not like other men—extortioners, unjust, adulterers, or even as this tax-collector. I fast twice a week; I give tithes of all that I possess." And the tax-collector, standing afar off, would not so much as raise his eyes to heaven, but beat his breast, saying, "God be merciful to me a sinner!" I tell you, this man went down to his house justified rather than the other; for everyone who exalts himself will be humbled, and he who humbles himself will be exalted.

(Luke 18:10–14)

Value of Membership in the Kingdom

❧

Treasure in a Field

Again, the kingdom of heaven is like treasure hidden in a field, which a man found and hid; and for joy over it he goes and sells all that he has and buys that field.

(Matthew 13:44)

The Pearl of Great Price

Again, the kingdom of heaven is like a merchant seeking beautiful pearls, who, when he had found one pearl of great price, went and sold all that he had and bought it.

(Matthew 13:45–46)

Treasures Old and New

Therefore every scribe instructed concerning the kingdom of heaven is like a householder who brings out of his treasure things new and old.

(Matthew 13:52)

Growth of the Kingdom

❧

The Mustard Seed

The kingdom of heaven is like a mustard seed, which a man took and sowed in his field, which indeed is the least of all the seeds; but when it is grown it is greater than the herbs and becomes a tree, so that the birds of the air come and nest in its branches.

(Matthew 13:31–32; cf. Mark 4:30–32, Luke 13:18–19)

Leaven

The kingdom of heaven is like leaven, which a woman took and hid in three measures of meal till it was all leavened.

(Matthew 13:33; cf. Luke 13:20–21)

Natural Growth

The kingdom of God is as if a man should scatter seed on the ground, and should sleep by night and rise by day, and the seed should sprout and grow, he himself does not know how. For the earth yields crops by itself: first the blade, then the head, after that the full grain in the head. But when the grain ripens, immediately he puts in the sickle, because the harvest has come.

(Mark 4:26–29)

Forgiveness

❧

The Unjust Servant

Therefore the kingdom of heaven is like a certain king who wanted to settle accounts with his servants. And when he had begun to settle accounts, one was brought to him who owed him ten thousand talents. But as he was not able to pay, his master commanded that he be sold, with his wife and children and all that he had, and that payment be made. The servant therefore fell down before him, saying, "Master, have patience with me, and I will pay you all." Then the master of that servant was moved with compassion, released him, and forgave him the debt. But that servant went out and found one of his fellow servants who owed him a hundred denarii; and he laid hands on him and took him by the throat, saying, "Pay me what you owe!" So his fellow servant fell down at his feet and begged him, saying, "Have patience with me, and I will pay you all." And he would not, but went and threw him into prison till he should pay the debt. So when his fellow servants saw what had been done, they were very grieved, and came and told their master all that had been done. Then his master, after he had called him, said to him, "You wicked servant! I forgave you all that debt because you begged me. Should you not also have had compassion on your fellow servant, just as I had pity on you?" And his master was angry, and delivered him to the torturers until he should pay all that was due to him. So My heavenly Father also will do to you if each of you, from his heart, does not forgive his brother his trespasses.

(Matthew 18:23–35)

Forgiven Much, Forgiven Little

There was a certain creditor who had two debtors. One owed five hundred denarii, and the other fifty. And when they had nothing with which to repay, he freely forgave them both. Tell Me, therefore, which of them will love him more? [*Simon answered and said, "I suppose the one whom he forgave more."*] You have rightly judged. [*And turning toward the woman, He said to Simon,*] Do you see this woman? I entered your house; you gave Me no water for My feet, but she has washed My feet with her tears and wiped them with the hair of her head. You gave Me no kiss, but this woman has not ceased to kiss My feet since the time I came in. You did not anoint My head with oil, but this woman has anointed My feet with fragrant oil. Therefore I say to you, her sins, which are many, are forgiven, for she loved much.

But to whom little is forgiven, the same loves little. (Luke 7:41–47)

The Prodigal Son

A certain man had two sons. And the younger of them said to his father, "Father, give me the portion of goods that falls to me." So he divided to them his livelihood. And not many days after, the younger son gathered all together, journeyed to a far country, and there wasted his possessions with prodigal living. But when he had spent all, there arose a severe famine in that land, and he began to be in want. Then he went and joined himself to a citizen of that country, and he sent him into his fields to feed swine. And he would gladly have filled his stomach with the pods that the swine ate, and no one gave him anything. But when he came to himself, he said, "How many of my father's hired servants have bread enough and to spare, and I perish with hunger! I will arise and go to my father, and will say to him, 'Father, I have sinned against heaven and before you, and I am no longer worthy to be called your son. Make me like one of your hired servants.'" And he arose and came to his father. But when he was still a great way off, his father saw him and had compassion, and ran and fell on his neck and kissed him. And the son said to him, "Father, I have sinned against heaven and in your sight, and am no longer worthy to be called your son." But the father said to his servants, "Bring out the best robe and put it on him, and put a ring on his hand and sandals on his feet. And bring the fatted calf here and kill it, and let us eat and be merry; for this my son was dead and is alive again; he was lost and is found." And they began to be merry. Now his older son was in the field. And as he came and drew near to the house, he heard music and dancing. So he called one of the servants and asked what these things meant. And he said to him, "Your brother has come, and because he has received him safe and sound, your father has killed the fatted calf." But he was angry and would not go in. Therefore his father came out and pleaded with him. So he answered and said to his father, "Lo, these many years I have been serving you; I never transgressed your commandment at any time; and yet you never gave me a young goat, that I might make merry with my friends. But as soon as this son of yours came, who has devoured your livelihood with harlots, you killed the fatted calf for him." And he said to him, "Son, you are always with me, and all that I have is yours. It was right that we should make merry and be glad, for your brother was dead and is alive again, and was lost and is found."

(Luke 15:11–32)

The Last Shall Be First

❧

The Laborer's Wages

For the kingdom of heaven is like a landowner who went out early in the morning to hire laborers for his vineyard. Now when he had agreed with the laborers for a denarius a day, he sent them into his vineyard. And he went out about the third hour and saw others standing idle in the marketplace, and said to them, "You also go into the vineyard, and whatever is right I will give you." So they went. Again he went out about the sixth and the ninth hour, and did likewise. And about the eleventh hour he went out and found others standing idle, and said to them, "Why have you been standing here idle all day?" They said to him, "Because no one hired us." He said to them, "You also go into the vineyard, and whatever is right you will receive." So when evening had come, the owner of the vineyard said to his steward, "Call the laborers and give them their wages, beginning with the last to the first." And when those came who were hired about the eleventh hour, they each received a denarius. But when the first came, they supposed that they would receive more; and they likewise received each a denarius. And when they had received it, they complained against the landowner, saying, "These last men have worked only one hour, and you made them equal to us who have borne the burden and the heat of the day." But he answered one of them and said, "Friend, I am doing you no wrong. Did you not agree with me for a denarius? Take what is yours and go your way. I wish to give to this last man the same as to you. Is it not lawful for me to do what I wish with my own things? Or is your eye evil because I am good?" So the last will be first, and the first last. For many are called, but few chosen.

(Matthew 20:1–16)

The Guests' Excuses

A certain man gave a great supper and invited many, and sent his servant at supper time to say to those who were invited, "Come, for all things are now ready." But they all with one accord began to make excuses. The first said to him, "I have bought a piece of ground, and I must go and see it. I ask you to have me excused." And another said, "I have bought five yoke of oxen, and I am going to test them. I ask you to have me excused." Still another said, "I have married a wife, and therefore I cannot come." So that servant came and reported these things to his master. Then the master of the house, being angry, said to his servant, "Go out quickly